Moving Learning Forward in Christian Schools

Moving Learning Forward in Christian Schools

A Practical Guide for a Mission-Focused Curriculum

Steven F. Butler

Foreword by Jay McTighe

Andy,
Thank you for
your interest in
Christian schools and
for your support.
Blessings,
Stev

RESOURCE *Publications* · Eugene, Oregon

Contents

List of Illustrations

List of Tables

Foreword

STEVEN BUTLER IS THE perfect author for this book. Indeed, one could view his long and rich career as an educator as the prewriting organizer! His diverse experiences in both public and Christian schools as a teacher, principal, assistant superintendent, university instructor, and educational consultant have afforded him a unique and an all-encompassing perspective across the educational spectrum.

The subtitle of the book, *A Mission-Focused Curriculum*, is noteworthy. Christian schools are inherently mission-driven. Yet, what does it mean to enact a mission-focused curriculum in the modern era? How should a Christian school's mission intersect with its concomitant commitment to develop competence in the academic disciplines as well as the twenty-first century skills of critical thinking, creativity, communication, and collaboration? How might a school collect evidence that it is fulfilling its mission—on both the spiritual and the academic strands?

The answers Butler offers are grounded by his extensive experience utilizing the Understanding by Design and Schooling by Design frameworks. These frameworks provide both the conceptual and practical infrastructures needed to build and implement a "guaranteed and viable" curriculum in Christian schools, and Butler effectively employs them to illustrate the path forward from the classroom to the boardroom.

Butler recognizes that lasting changes in schools will only be realized through systems thinking and coordinated actions. Accordingly, he addresses the topic systemically by describing the curriculum components, assessment system, pedagogical practices, professional development, and school structures necessary to achieve mission accomplished. He cites relevant research with the assurance of an academic while offering practical advice with the clarity and confidence of a veteran educator.

Foreword

While the catalogs of educational publishers are flooded with books on educational leadership, few are focused so precisely on the culture and context of contemporary Christian schools, and none addresses the type of curriculum needed to help them realize their historic mission. Accordingly, your mission is to read this book and heed its sound recommendations. Your entire educational community—staff, students, and parents—will reap the benefits.

Jay McTighe

Acknowledgments

Writing a book is a team effort. The writing of this book has involved many people, all of whom have made important contributions.

I would first like to thank my wife, Karen, whose encouragement over the years has allowed me to participate in a wide variety of rich educational experiences, which led to my belief that education is a worthy profession and that Christian education has a special place in God's kingdom. Also, being an English major, she has been a wonderful first editor.

Pastor Bill Douglas provided me with insights from a non-educator perspective, adding good suggestions for tying the ideas to biblical underpinnings.

Over the years, Doug and Lanetta Ward have consistently encouraged me to continue in this work even in times when it would have been easy to set it aside. Their belief that the quality of Christian education can be improved and their faith and trust in this work have made a significant difference.

Libby Gontarz's editorial work was both timely and exceptional. Her professional experience as an educator, writer, and editor was a perfect match assisting me through the challenges of preparing the final manuscript. Also, thank you to Judy Wilson for her detailed proofing of the final product.

A thank you to Matthew Wimer, the Editorial Production Manager at Wipf and Stock Publishers, for his patient support in guiding me through the myriad of publishing details.

I have worked in or with both public and Christian schools and colleges but have always had a special place in my heart for Christian schools. Two Christian K–12 schools, Three Rivers Christian School in Longview, Washington, and Grace Cascade Christian School in Medford, Oregon, have been willing partners in the writing of this book. You will find numerous documents from their school improvement journeys in this book. It has been a joy watching them during the change process required for school improvement. The times of revelation, discussions, decision-making, and struggles have contributed to their teachers' professional growth and improved student learning. I am grateful for the two superintendents, Erin Hart and Dr. Ken Townsend, for their courageous leadership in their respective schools and their willingness to contribute generously to the book, including being beta readers.

Most importantly, I would like to thank Jay McTighe and the late Grant Wiggins for their work over the years in encouraging educators to be principled and thoughtful about their pedagogy and practices. I owe deep gratitude to Jay McTighe for the numerous trainings that I have had the privilege to attend and for his work with the schools and university within my sphere. He has helped craft many of my beliefs about education. Jay McTighe's support in writing this book, which is specifically focused on Christian schools, was remarkable.

Introduction

MUCH HAS BEEN WRITTEN about being a mission-driven organization, both in business and industry and in education circles. Today, nearly every school and district has guiding mission and vision statements. The importance of a mission is valid. The real challenge is operationalizing the mission. To use a common phrase, the devil is in the details.

This book outlines an approach to enable K–12 Christian schools to be more attentive to becoming mission-driven organizations. Each Christian school is unique. A region's characteristics (politics, ethnic makeup, economics, weather, geography, and spiritual heritage) impact its culture. Consequently, a Christian school invariably adapts to its community's needs and features. This results in each Christian school having specific interests that it wishes to fulfill.

The desire to develop spiritually grounded young men and women for the furtherance of God's kingdom is common to Christian schools. This is the primary task that separates public and private schools from Christian schools. Using Grant Wiggins and Jay McTighe's Understanding by Design® and Schooling by Design frameworks, the ideas presented here concentrate on this foundational element of a Christian school's mission.

Leaders of Christian schools should be regularly asking themselves crucial questions that keep them focused on their mission:

- What evidence do we have that our students are fulfilling our mission?

- Does our instructional program align with our mission?

- Do our personnel practices result in hiring, training, and keeping staff who support our school's mission?

- Does the Christian school's board and leadership consistently make decisions and act in ways that support the school's mission?

- Do the Christian school's policies, structures, and resources readily sustain the mission?

The hope is that this book will stimulate thinking, conversation, and action of Christian school leaders in order to improve the quality of their schools by being more mission-aligned.

1

To Change or Not to Change, That Is the Question

The test of education is if students are taught the things they had to know to deal with an uncontrollably changing world.

—HENRY ADAM, HARVARD CLASS OF 1858

As THE WORLD HURTLES forward, Christian schools face the inevitable question: What do we hold on to, and what do we need to change in our school? This question arises when considering mission and vision, governance structure, finances, facilities, staffing, student population, and the instructional program.

Over the last twenty years, many Christian schools in the United States have been struggling to maintain enrollment and, in all too many cases, have been closing the doors of their Christ-centered education ministry to their communities. Since 2005, Christian schools have been closing at a rate of 150 per year.[1] The top eleven evangelical Christian school associations in the United States have suffered some level of decline during the past decade, aggregately decreasing in school membership from 8,064 schools in the 2006 school year to 6,484 in the 2012 school year.[2]

1. Nichols, "Schools at Risk," 18.
2. Nichols, "Schools at Risk," 17–18.

Moving Learning Forward in Christian Schools

Christian schools in Western nations are facing
significant threats to sustainability and relevance.

—LYNN E. SWANER, DAN BEERENS, AND ERIK ELLEFSEN,
Mindshift: Catallizing Change in Christian Education, 2019

Studies conducted at California Baptist University[3] and Regent University[4] explored why Christian schools close. Both studies revealed a strong link between Christian school closures and failed leadership. In fact, of all contributing factors, failed leadership was identified as the greatest single cause of Christian school closures among ACSI member schools, both church-sponsored and independent. Changes in culture was the second most important influence.

In the 2018 article "Now or Never: The Research Basis for Innovation in Christian Schools," Vance Nichols wrote that the key to both leadership failure and cultural change was the seeming inability—or unwillingness—of Christian schools to adapt and change to the shifting social and educational landscape in the United States. Ritzema predicted in 2013 using prophetic-sounding terms that unless Christian schools—meaning Christian school leaders—take note of the changing cultural, educational, and technological landscape of the twenty-first century and take action by innovating, retooling, and reinventing themselves, schools would continue to close.[5]

Underscoring this reality, Gene Frost, retired head of school at Wheaton Academy, found that one of the problems endangering Christian schools is the stubborn determination to perpetuate the status quo rather than using inspiration to build the future by being creative and innovative while staying true to core Christian beliefs. He asserted that resisting educational innovation by hiding behind the misguided notion that remaining the same will preserve a school's values only hastens decline. Failure to embrace new educational practices that can stimulate progress will prevent essential growth.[6]

Many people believe that economic pressures are the main reason Christian schools close their doors. Financial challenges certainly are a factor; but it could be argued that there were significant economic challenges

---

3. Nichols, "Schools at Risk," 17–18.

4. Fitzpatrick, *Why Schools Close.*

5. Ritzema, Regional Director's Report presentation.

6. Frost, *Does Your Christian School,* 7.

during the 1970s, when inflation was very high, yet Christian schools were opening and flourishing at a remarkable rate. The 1970s and 1980s period would now be considered the height of popularity of Christian schools in the United States.

Certainly, understanding the times (economic and technological impact, culture, spiritual conditions, and educational landscape) is important for Christian school leaders as they grapple with the question of change in their schools. Is the model that Christian schools followed during the heyday of the 1970s and 1980s adequate or appropriate for today?

Historical Overview of Education

Considering the current situation in education today can shed some light on issues and practices that are worthy of consideration when instituting changes. Historically, there have always been voices calling for change in education. There have been a number of reform efforts attempted in American education as a response to the changes in how we live and work. The options for change in education are plentiful. The variety of books, articles, conferences, webinars, podcasts, internet sites, and consultants is overwhelming.

The last generation has seen three major reform movements, beginning in the early 1980s. The impact of technology and the resulting shrinking, interconnected world began to shift the economic and social networks. A gap began to occur between what schools were doing and the needs of business and industry. Since the 1980s, the needs of business and industry have dominated the voices calling for change in education.

- After the *A Nation at Risk* report in 1982, with its characterization of the state of education being "a tide of mediocrity," the excellence movement ensued. This was a top-down undertaking that called for more homework, more rigorous courses, more credits for high school graduation, more tests, and more expectations of teachers than in the past.

- This was quickly followed in the 1990s by the site-based management movement, a bottom-up restructuring, in which schools were given significant control over staffing and budgets, and schools emphasized shared decision-making, shared planning time, and heterogeneous groupings.

- The current top-down reform undertaking, the standards-based movement, has lingered for over twenty years. During this time, academic content standards were adopted in all fifty states in the late 1990s and were quickly followed by statewide assessments. The federal government entered into the reform arena in 2002 using the No Child Left Behind legislation as leverage in an attempt to improve student academic performance.

Now after forty years of efforts (which have included governors' summits; state and federal legislation; hundreds of writing committees; extensive test development and implementation; thousands of teacher conferences, workshops, and trainings; countless national reports; and incredible amounts of money spent), there has been only a nominal change in student academic performance in this country.

With all this going on in America and in the public education systems, how should Christian schools respond?

The Purpose of Education

Most people view the purpose of school from one of four spheres:

- intellectual purposes such as the development of mathematical and reading skills
- political purposes such as the assimilation of immigrants or developing educated voting constituents
- economic purposes such as job preparation or being competitive in a world market
- social purposes such as the development of social and moral responsibility

Over the last generation, the economic lens (developing an effective twenty-first century workforce) has dominated the educational landscape in the United States. There has been an untold number of books, articles, and reports written outlining the characteristics of the modern employee. Many lists of characteristics have been generated. Here are a few examples.

Workplace Know-How

Competencies. Effective workers can productively use

- Resources: allocating time, money, materials, space, and staff;
- Interpersonal Skills: working on teams, teaching others, serving customers, leading, negotiating, and working well with people from culturally diverse backgrounds;
- Information: acquiring and evaluating data, organizing and maintaining files, interpreting and communicating, and using computers to process information;
- Systems: understanding social, organizational, and technological systems, monitoring and correcting performance, and designing or improving systems;
- Technology: selecting equipment and tools, applying technology to specific tasks, and maintaining and troubleshooting technologies.

The Foundation. Competence requires

- Basic Skills: reading, writing, arithmetic and mathematics, speaking and listening;
- Thinking Skills: thinking creatively, making decisions, solving problems, seeing things in the mind's eye, knowing how to learn, and reasoning;
- Personal Qualities: individual responsibility, self-esteem, sociability, self-management, and integrity.

What Work Requires of Schools: A SCANS Report for America 2000. Department of Labor, Washington DC. The Secretary's Commission on Achieving Necessary Skills, 1991.

Seven Survival Skills

1. Critical thinking and problem solving
2. Collaboration across networks and leading by example
3. Agility and adaptability
4. Initiative and entrepreneurship
5. Effective oral, written, and multimedia communication
6. Accessing and analyzing information
7. Curiosity and imagination

Adapted from Tony Wagner, *The Global Achievement Gap*, 2008.

Employability Skills

Applied Knowledge

- Applied Academic Skills
- Critical Thinking Skills

Workplace Skills

- Information Use
- Communication Skills
- Systems Thinking
- Technology Use

Effective Relationships

- Interpersonal Skills
- Personal Qualities

Employability Skills Framework, Career and Technical Education, 2013.

Interestingly, many of the desired characteristics are nonacademic qualities, or "soft skills." While the changing world has caused a need for numerous nonacademic skills, the legislated approach to creating twenty-first century workers has been a knowledge- and skills-focused schooling with an emphasis on standardized multiple-choice tests. The struggle between the two areas is obvious and has resulted in a regular expression of frustration from business and industry about young people entering the workforce and from educators who believe that education should serve more than the economic needs of our country.

> Virtue is much harder to develop than skill, and it takes
> much longer. But the payoff is much greater.
> —MARK BATTERSON

In addition, the standards that have been written have numerous issues:

- There are too many standards than can be effectively taught in a traditional K–12 setting.
- The standards are often either too broad or too specific.
- The language in the standards is at times vague and open to much interpretation.
- The standards focus primarily on skills and knowledge acquisition and very little on understanding or transfer of learning.

Schools have been placed in an impossible position, trying to teach an excessive number of content standards to appease state and federal mandates and having to give up some content-focused instruction for the sake of working on the needed soft skills of business and industry. Dr. Robert Marzano, a leading researcher in education, has stated that in order to cover all the content required in many states' standards, schooling would need to be changed from K–12 to K-22.[7]

For Christian schools, none of the four typical purposes (intellectual, political, economic, and social) of education is their primary one. Christian schools' most significant purpose is the spiritual development of students. They generally do include intellectual, political, economic, and social purposes in their goals; however, they are clearly different from

---

7. Scherer, *How and Why Standards*, 15.

public and other independent private schools because of this critical difference in emphasis.

> Education without values, as useful as it is,
> seems rather to make a man a clever devil.
>
> —C.S. LEWIS

Key Chapter Takeaways

✓ Change is difficult for human beings, including educators.

✓ The current climate and culture of the world impacts Christian schools. This includes the current trends within education, which focus on the needs of business and industry.

✓ The expectations that are imposed on education today have both changed and exceeded those from prior generations.

✓ Christian schools today are facing challenging times with regards to what to keep from the past and changes needed to best equip young men and women to be godly servants for Christ.

Concluding Thoughts

Knowing that there are limits on what can be expected of any school, what needs to change and what should a Christian school focus on? This is a key question for Christian school leadership. Although change is difficult for organizations and the individuals within them, understanding what current brain research is revealing about how the brain learns could be a motivator for change.

The nonprofit institution is not merely delivering a service.
It wants the end user to be not a user but a *doer*. It uses a service
to bring about a change in a human being. In that sense, a school, for
instance, is quite different from Proctor & Gamble. It creates habits,
vision, commitment . . . It attempts to become part of the recipient
rather than merely a supplier. Until this has happened the nonprofit
institution has had no results; it has only good intentions.

—PETER DRUCKER

Moving Learning Forward in Christian Schools

Educator Interview

Q: You have a unique perspective of Christian schools because of your background of serving in Christian schools and as regional director for ACSI. Do you feel there is a need for Christian schools to make changes to meet the needs of the twenty-first century?

A: Yes, change is needed. Today, knowledge is immediately available from a smartphone. Most students rely on short-term memory and cram for tests hoping for a good grade. Afterward, they may be fortunate to retain half of what they learned. Contrast this with understanding the content and transferring this understanding to new, relevant issues where retention is closer to 90 percent.

Superintendent

KEN TOWNSEND

Bio

Christian School Teacher
Christian School Principal
Christian School Superintendent
ASCI Northwest Regional Director

BA, Grace College
MA, Talbot Theological Seminary
EdD, Pepperdine University

Additionally, education is perpetually changing, as are jobs. We can no longer prepare students for vocations that may soon disappear. Instead, we must teach them to innovate, to work collaboratively, to solve problems, and to become more entrepreneurial—all through a biblical lens and Christian worldview.

Q: In Vance Nichols's 2018 article "Now or Never: The Research Basis for Innovation in Christian Schools," he stated that the number-one reason for Christian schools having to close their doors was the lack of leadership. As you have observed many Christian schools, have you found this to be true? Are there other significant reasons?

A: Yes, I agree with Vance Nichols's position. I know that leadership is a significant factor, but there are other issues. The best leaders know how to woo others toward a vision and can balance tasks and people as mutual priorities. Leaders welcome input and evaluation from advocates and "enemies." Possessing multiple thoughts about policies, processes, or products allows for a deeper and richer implementation. Not many view conflict as an opportunity to add facets to the diamond of wisdom.

Strong leaders can mitigate difficulties, but Christian schools face challenges unrelated to leadership, too. The price of education never goes down, so pricing tuition to be affordable is a huge mistake. Instead, schools need to charge what it costs and provide scholarships for those in need. Otherwise, we are providing scholarships for everyone, which hurts the school. Donors will fatigue giving to a bottomless leech. Schools must operate as both a ministry and a business by offering value, not minimal cost; by modeling stewardship, not ownership; by being entrepreneurial, not status quo.

Boards of Christian schools need training, too. Too many boards are administrative and interfere with leadership or too quickly release their head of school instead of investing in them. Boards and subordinates tend to focus on the discrepant instead of the areas of strength and believe a new leader is the answer. A change in leadership can set an organization back several years and is oftentimes more costly than working with existing staff, adjusting job responsibilities, and/or delegating tasks. Another challenge is the church-school relationship: Sharing facilities and equipment with different needs and priorities, competing visions, unclear leadership, and financial responsibilities make going solo seem more attractive.

Q: You are currently serving as a Christian school superintendent and are trying to make impactful changes to the instructional program. How has this unfolded for you and your staff? What are the positive results and/or challenges? Have you been able to keep your mission your focus in this process?

A: Yes, we started with our mission and from the mission derived our student outcomes. We then spent time identifying ways to measure these outcomes so we could know if we were making progress and how best to correct our course if we were not moving in the right direction. We collaboratively identified the essential research-based learning principles so our teachers went into the classroom well aware and had agreement of how learning best occurs. Then we incorporated principles from Understanding by Design and are looking at Schooling by Design.

The response has been exciting. At first, teachers were thinking this was one more novel idea everyone would soon forget. Now, they are understanding this is a shift in culture and a way to align learning with current brain research. By focusing on enduring understandings and by using essential questions, we are witnessing a heightened love of learning among the students. I am excited about the future.

Q: What do you see as needed changes in Christian schools' instructional programs for them to be the most impactful for God's kingdom?

A: I believe that God has designed every person uniquely in God's image. Each has unique spiritual gifts, passions, abilities, personalities, strengths, and experiences. If we can teach each in a manner that addresses these unique qualities, we will be teaching as God desires. We cannot separate sacred and secular, rather must see all learners as designed by God for his purpose and serving in their areas of passion, strength, and ability as God intends. This means everyone is in ministry. As we align instruction with brain research and teach through a biblical lens by transferring a Christian worldview while targeting each learner's passion, we will have the best of Christian instructional programs.

Many Christian schools lack the financial resources to serve all of God's children. This will likely remain a tension between ideal and real.

Q: What advice would you give to other Christian school administrators who are desiring to make significant changes in their Christian school's instructional program?

A: I would encourage Christian school administrators to explore the principles of Understanding by Design. I would also encourage them to seek an instructional coach who can help with strategy, focus, and implementation. A coach can help keep Christian school administrators on track and making the progress essential for success. I would also remind them our battle is not against flesh and blood but against the principalities and powers of the air. We must stay on our knees and in God's Word to find the power necessary for the day's demands. God is faithful to provide wisdom, strength, and endurance!

2

The Impact of Current Brain Research

The difference between novices and experts in a field appears to be that experts tend (because of a great deal of experience in a field) to organize information into much larger chunks, while novices work with isolated bits of information.

—BENJAMIN BLOOM

Brain Research and Cognition

INTERESTINGLY, DURING THIS SAME period from the 1980s, the work of neuroscientists and cognitive psychologists has revealed many insights into how the human brain learns best. This knowledge has seemed to exist in a parallel universe, as there is little intersection between the politically legislated world of public education and the research-based knowledge regarding teaching and learning practices. In particular, recent brain research has discovered that learning occurs best when organized around bigger ideas.

In addition, many things that we thought were true about how the brain works are not true. Below is a list of once-accepted ideas that we know now are false premises:

- You cannot control how your brain grows.
- The brain does not grow brain cells by the time students reach secondary level.

- Connections between neurons are relatively fixed throughout your life.

- Some people are more left-brain and others right-brain thinkers.

- You use only about 10 percent of your brain.

- Individuals learn better when they receive information in their preferred learning style.

- Older adults can't learn as well as young people.

- Emotions are a proven distraction from learning and should be kept apart from cognitive thinking.

- Our brains are able to multitask.

- Our brains shut down when we sleep.

- Students should be praised for achievement rather than for their effort.

- Erratic teenage behaviors are a result of hormonal changes.[1]

In *Teaching with the Brain in Mind,* Eric Jensen notes that we have learned that the human brain does grow new neurons and that genes are not fixed.[2] There is a delicate interplay between emotional states and cognition.[3] Music can affect cognition.[4] Exercise is strongly correlated with increased brain mass, better cognition, mood regulation, and new cell growth.[5] Teen behavior is a result of a complex array of fast-changing factors—not just hormones.[6]

Neurologists have found that the brain is much more flexible and adaptable than we once thought. The benefits of this neuroplasticity are the brain is continually resculpting itself in response to experience and learning. New brain cells do form throughout life. The brain's emotional circuitry matures and becomes more balanced with age. The brain's two hemispheres are more equally used by older adults. Deliberate effort—working harder and smarter—can influence the types of changes in the brain that take place.

---

1. For more information about current brain research, see the Human Brain Project. www.humanbrainproject.eu

2. Jensen, *Teaching with Brain*, 11.

3. Jensen, *Teaching with Brain*, 68.

4. Jensen, *Teaching with Brain*, 12, 14.

5. Jensen, *Teaching with Brain*, 60, 62.

6. Jensen, *Teaching with Brain*, 30.

Teachers' beliefs, teaching practices, assessment practices,
study habits, the design of schools, the structure of the school day,
the social and emotional environment of the school—all these
factors influence how students' brains get rewired, whether we seek
to deliberately manage these factors or not.

—WHITMAN AND KELLEHER,
Neuroteach: Brain Science and the Future of Education

Gene Cohen states that fluid intelligence is on-the-spot reasoning ability—the raw mental agility that doesn't depend completely on prior learning.[7] This is the speed with which information can be analyzed as well as a measurement of attention and memory capacity. This is the type of native intelligence that IQ tests strive (not always successfully) to measure. Crystallized intelligence, on the other hand, is accumulated information and vocabulary acquired from school and everyday life. It encompasses the application of skills and knowledge to solving problems. Many studies have shown that fluid intelligence slowly declines with age, whereas crystallized intelligence often improves or expands.

Cohen also notes:

> Some people believe mental ability is "all in the genes." Genes, of course, are very powerful and broadly speaking, the genes we inherit do set some limits on what we can achieve mentally and physically. Rather than constituting an immutable blueprint for our bodies and behavior, genes, it turns out, are highly sensitive to our environment—what we are exposed to, what we perceive, the emotions we feel, the stress we are under, and a host of other factors in our lives. Many genes include 'switches' for their activity; they can be turned on or off, or their activity levels dialed up or down like a volume control.[8]

It used to be assumed that high levels of achievement at any time of life were mostly a result of luck and genes, with effort only a small part of it all. But it turns out that continued success has much less to do with inborn genius and more to do with deliberate practice. This practice is a commitment to working at a skill repeatedly while meticulously zeroing in on faults, the kind of strategic practice that can work at any age.

7. Cohen, *Mature* Mind, 111.
8. Cohen, *Mature* Mind, 9.

Pulitzer Prize-winning science writer Barbara Strauch writes,

> Contrary to stereotypical views of intelligence and the naive theo-
> ries of many educated laypersons, young adulthood is not the de-
> velopmental period of peak cognitive functioning for many of the
> higher-order cognitive abilities. In four of the six abilities studied
> (vocabulary, verbal memory, spatial orientation, inductive reason-
> ing), middle-aged individuals (ages 40–65) are functioning at a
> higher level than they did at age 25.[9]

Just because you are old doesn't mean you have used up your brain's
memory system. We are limited only by the time we have in life for learning. Our brains (as long as they are healthy) could contain many lifetimes
of information. Our brains contain billions of neurons, which is why the
brain's memory capacity is essentially limitless.

Education is the best provision for old age.

—ARISTOTLE

Education and literacy levels impact how well the brain ages. Education is more important than social standing and obliterates the impact of
income. People with the lack of or low levels of education are more likely to
develop dementia and Alzheimer's.

In Harvard University and University of Florida studies it was determined that the most decisive factor that predicted wisdom was the level of
self-centeredness. It was those who focused on something outside themselves who turned out to be the wisest. Those who scored high in wisdom
also scored very low on self-centeredness. They cared for others.[10]

Being able to see complex issues from multiple perspectives and having empathy for others are characteristics foundational to wisdom. Both of
these attributes are consistent with Christlike character.

The Importance of Teachers

In Whitman and Kelleher's book *Neuroteach: Brain Science and the Future
of Education*, the authors note that teachers are in the business of changing

9. Strauch, *Secret Life*, 14.
10. Strauch, *Secret Life*, 45–46.

brains, and recent research in cognitive science, neuroscience, and behavioral psychology has given educators new insights into how students learn.[11] What has been learned is not the answer to all educational challenges, but cognitive science and neuroscience research have implications for educators.

Because students spend between 12,000 and 15,000 hours under the direct influence of school and the staff, educators must pay attention to how they ask students to spend time in school. Sadly, many teachers lack an understanding of how the brain receives, filters, consolidates, and applies learning for both the short term and long term.

Brain Research and Memory

Better understanding of how memory works in the human brain helps educators better cultivate memory. There is an erroneous and popular concept of the brain that it records or videotapes life like a digital recording device. The reality is very different. There is no single, all-purpose resting location for all memories. Our best learning and recall involve multiple memory locations and systems.[12]

In general, memories seem to be encoded in the areas of the brain that originally processed them.[13] The fact is that memory resides in many different locations of the brain. When we recall memories, our brain has to reconstruct the fragmented Humpty Dumpty memory pieces.[14]

To learn, we must remember. Memories, in turn, are created when clusters of hundreds or thousands of neurons fire in a unique pattern. The process of memory formation is summarized by the phrase "Neurons that fire together, wire together."

There are certain types of memories that people are naturally very good at because they are related to survival:

- locations
- procedures
- emotional experiences
- conditioned response

11. Whitman and Kelleher, *Neuroteach*, 1.

12. Schacter, "Priming," 252–53.

13. Moscovitch, "Recovered Consciousness," 276.

14. Shimamura, *Relational Binding*, 61–72; cited in Jensen, *Teaching with Brain*, 130.

Learning involves multiple stages of processing through different portions of the brain. These structures act as a surge protector for the brain. The hippocampus actually inhibits speeds of processing and serves as a gating device.

Because the brain limits how much information can be retained at one time, expanding the amount of content that students are exposed to only benefits language acquisition. You can teach more and faster, but students will simply forget more and faster. The hippocampus learns fast but has a very small memory capacity.[15] The organization and distribution of memory in the hippocampus takes time, and much of this work occurs while we sleep. Most encoding, regardless of the location in the brain, is enhanced by a good night's sleep. The more complex the learning, the more helpful sleep is.[16]

Teaching without an awareness of how the brain learns is like designing a glove with no sense of what a hand looks like. If classrooms are to be places of learning, then the brain—organ of learning—must be understood and accommodated.

—LESLIE A. HART

In-depth learning requires time for organizing, integrating, and storing new information. Even visual images require rest time for processing.[17] The physical process of building connections for explicit learning begins within fifteen minutes of exposure to new information. This consolidation takes time and is just one more limitation on the speed of the learning process. They continue to strengthen over the next hour, and it takes up to six hours to complete formation of the synaptic connection for implicit learning.[18] The new learning must imprint, and if the synapse is disturbed during this time, the memory is lost. The brain must recycle proteins in the neurons that are crucial to long-term memory formation. To help accomplish this, an incubation or settling time is necessary for new learning to take place.[19] This means that learning improves with short sessions and rest

---

15. Kelso, *Dynamic Patterns*, 334.

16. Piegneux et al., "Sleeping Brain," 111–24; cited in Jensen, *Teaching with Brain*, 130.

17. Stickgold, "Visual discrimination," 1237–238.

18. Goda, Mechanism of synapse, 243.

19. Schroth, "Effects of delay," 78–82; cited in Jensen, *Teaching with Brain*, 130.

intervals versus constant new material. It is also dependent on frequent sleep for recycling of the learning.[20]

THE SCHEDULE FOR COMPLEX LEARNING

STAGE ONE
15 MINS

Initial connection is made. Synapses are formed or modified within the first fifteen minutes.

STAGE TWO
60 MINS

Most explicit learning is held for evaluation by the hippocampus. Synaptic adhesion strengthens.

STAGE THREE
1-3 DAYS

At night, new learning is organized and codified. The hippocampus distributes it to the cortex through neural repetition for long-term storage.

STAGE FOUR
3-30 DAYS

Integration into related networks may occur with appropriate stimulation.

Based on data from Goda & Davis, 2003 and Sejnowsk, 2002.

The bottom line is that learning connections take time and maintenance.[21]

In many schools, the curriculum is too wide and shallow. Many teachers who complain of having to do so much reteaching are the same ones trying to cram too much content into too little time. Less is more when it

---

20. Bodizs, "Sleep-dependent," 441–57; cited in Jensen, *Teaching with Brain*, 130.

21. Sanes and Lichtman, "Induction, Assembly," 791–805; cited in Jensen, *Teaching with Brain*, 130.

comes to making memory. Trying to teach too much and too fast results in learning that does not last.

"'I learn it for the test and then immediately forget it.' There is a not-too-subtle clue that something is wrong with 'learning' as we tend to witness and perpetrate it."[22] The idea that current accessibility is not a reliable index of learning has profound implications in how we craft the flow of the school year and how we assess learning.[23]

Facts that are memorized by repetitive rehearsal, without context or relationship connections, are stored in a more remote area of the brain and are more difficult to retrieve. The goal of research-based education is to structure lessons to ultimately rely less on rote memory. Helping students access and use more effective types of memory storage and retrieval will literally change student brains.

Variations on Repetition

Activity	When to do it
Pre-exposure	Days, weeks, months, years ahead (covert)
Previewing	Minutes, hours ahead (overt coming attractions)
Priming	Seconds, minutes (overt exposure)
Reviewing	Minutes after learning (overt)
Revision	Hours, days, weeks later (overt)

Eric Jensen, *Teaching with the Brain in Mind,* p. 39

Rehearsal is the processing of information, which allows us to hold the data in consciousness (working memory) for longer than a few seconds and to work with the information in such a way as to ensure its transfer to long-term memory. There are two major types of rehearsal strategies:

1. Rote rehearsal—deliberate, continual repetition of material in the same form in which it entered working memory

22. Whitman and Kelleher, *Neuroteach,* 80.

23. Clark and Bjork, "When and Why," 21–22.

2. Elaborative rehearsal—elaborating or integrating information, giving it some kind of meaning, creating chunks of reminders

> As students develop their skills of observing, discriminating patterns and details, and making connections, they are at a higher cognitive level, which stimulates and interconnects more of the brain's memory circuitry. Eventually, new dendrite sprouts will grow and root the new information into the long-term memory storage banks.[24]

Either you have your learners' attention, or they can be making meaning, but never both at the same time. Meaning is generated internally, and it takes time. External input (more content) conflicts with the processing of prior content. Students rarely get training in how to be calm, thoughtful, or reflective, and they are given little time to practice these skills in class.

In Christian schools, providing students with time to read, study, and meditate on the Bible provides opportunity to rewire their brains to align with God's Word. The result is that student decision-making and actions are more likely to be consistent with God's principles. Often students spend much of their time on survey-knowledge Bible courses with little time spent on studying for understanding along with reflective writing. Taking time to grapple with godly principles and/or meditating on God's Word provides the opportunity for the brain to engage in deeper thinking about the Scriptures.

Long-term memory is really a bit of a misnomer because it implies a single storage location in the brain. In fact, long-term memories are distributed all across the brain. This is not only a very efficient system for the brain, but it also helps protect the brain from catastrophic memory loss.

There are numerous brain-based strategies to consolidate learned material into long-term memory:

- Introduce the most significant information when students are engaged with focused attention.

- Include repeated practice of accurate and precise observation techniques in a meaningful context.

- Use multisensory avenues of exposure to the information.

- Create student-centered, personal motivation for learning.

24. Willis, *Research-based Strategies*, 15–16.

- Have students use the learning to answer personally relevant, critical-thinking questions.

- Have students make and support judgments using the new knowledge.

- Have students determine ways to use the information outside of school.

- Have students make ongoing observations and continually revise/refine their hypothesis.

- Have students analyze and compare their work and the work of experts.

- Have students use KWL charts and graphic organizers.

- Engage students with open-ended questions that are focused on enduring understandings and "big ideas."[25]

- Use authentic assessments to get at students' level of understanding.

- Provide students opportunity for reflection and metacognition.

- Provide multiple exposures to the same or similar information over time.

Memories that are well integrated into the context of other memories are more resistant to degradation than memories of specific details or facts not linked to other memories. Working memory and the episodic form of declarative memory can degrade over time; semantic and procedural memories are quite stable.

Engaging in the process of learning actually increases one's capacity to learn. Some strategies that increase transfer of learning from working memory to long-term memory:

- using multiple senses

- novel and/or unexpected events

- thought-provoking questions

- experiential learning

- emotionally significant events

- relating learning to previous learning

- relationships and/or patterns.

---

25. Enduring understandings and "big ideas" are terminology used in *Understanding by Design*. Full discussion of these terms is found in Chapter 3, section "Big Ideas."

The Brain and Physical Activity

The part of the brain that processes movement is the same part of the brain that processes learning. There are strong connections between movement—physical education, breaks, recess, energizing activities—and improved cognition. Exercise fuels the brain with oxygen, but it also feeds it neurotrophins (high-nutrient chemical "packages") to increase the number of connections between neurons.

Exercise is known to increase the baseline of new neuron growth. Students who are engaged in daily physical education programs consistently show not just superior motor fitness but also better academic performance and a better attitude toward school.[26] The relationship between movement and learning is so strong that it pervades all of life, not just for young children.

In addition to physical education and recess, some ideas for the use of movement in the classroom are

- drama and role plays;
- quick games;
- stretching and arm and leg crossovers;
- walkabouts; and
- across-the-room share pairs.

Weaving movement, drama, and the arts into mathematics, geography, social skills, science, and English-language arts can benefit cognition.

Rest, Sleep, and Learning

Every brain needs periodic rests during which neurotransmitters can be replenished and executive function can process the new material. Neurotransmitters rebuild in minutes if students are given a short break before they are severely depleted. During these rests, the newly learned material has the opportunity to go from working, or short-term, memory into relational memory. During sleep, frontal lobe activity (executive functions) is considerably reduced. This allows the brain the opportunity to rehearse learned material, sometimes in dreams. While sleeping, the brain is least distracted by sensory input, which bombards it during the day; therefore,

26. Donovan, "Plasma B-endorphin," 231.

it can devote a greater portion of its energy to organizing and filing the memories from the day. Sleep helps the brain consolidate and cement new knowledge and experience into memory.

> Memory storage in the brain is most efficient during the longest periods of uninterrupted deep sleep rather than during the dream sleep . . . This period of deep sleep is a critical time when the brain transforms recent memories into long-term memories by building and extending the dendrite branches . . . This recognition of the need for sleep time from six or less to eight hours can increase memory and alertness up to 25 percent.[27]

Teenagers can have a hard time sleeping. At about 7:30 p.m., a teen feels wide awake and fully alert, unlike an adult who is starting to wind down and feel sleepier as the evening progresses. At 10 p.m., the adult is ready to go to bed, whereas teenagers' wind-down time takes place much later.

Adolescents need nine hours and fifteen minutes of sleep. Children need ten hours, and adults need an hour less than adolescents. Teens rarely get that much sleep due to early school start time, inability to fall asleep until late at night, work, social life, and homework. Most teens are chronically sleep deprived and try to catch up on their sleep by sleeping late on the weekends. Optimally, teens should go to bed and wake up at the same time each day.

Sleep deprivation can impair memory and inhibit creativity, making it difficult for sleep-deprived students to learn. Teens struggle to learn to deal with stress and how to control their emotions, and sleep deprivation makes it even more difficult. Irritability, lack of self-confidence, and mood swings are common in teens, but sleep deprivation makes these things worse. Teenagers' judgment can be impaired.[28]

Emotions, Stress, Anxiety, and Learning

Emotions, thinking, and learning are interconnected. Emotions are one of the most important regulators of learning and memory. Moderate stress is an ally in encoding learning but not in retrieving it.[29]

---

27. Frank, Issa, Stryker, "Sleep Enhances Plasticity," 275.
28. Dement, "Adolescent Sleep."
29. Cahill et al., "Enhanced Human Memory," 271–72.

Negative emotional events are recalled longer and affect more brain circuits. Positive emotional events also get priority for memory. Brain chemicals (cortisol, norepinephrine, and dopamine) support improved memory. They are released under predictable conditions such as risk, excitement, urgency, and pleasure.

Emotions drive attention, create meaning, and have their own memory pathways.[30] The impact of emotions

- constitutes the passion for learning;
- helps orchestrate attention priorities;
- supports either persistence or retreat;
- allows us to enjoy and celebrate learning;
- evokes necessary empathy, support, or fear; and
- associates learning with either pain or pleasure.

> Many more nerve fibers run from the limbic system up to the cortex than run from the cortex back down to the limbic system. If neural activity were water, the limbic system would have a fire-hose connection to the cortex and a straw connection from the cortex. This fundamental imbalance in connectivity means that emotions can easily overwhelm and overrule thinking, deliberating parts of our brain . . . this basic imbalance between reason and emotion leads to all sorts of trouble. Our frequent inability to control our emotions and cravings is one of the defining features of our species. Our ability to control our emotions and modulate our behavior appropriately, however, is a hallmark of maturity.[31]

Emotions affect student behavior because they create distinct mind-body states. The presence of dozens of chemicals in the body dramatically alters a person's frame of mind. Teachers who help their students feel good about their learning through classroom success, friendships, and celebrations are doing the very things the student brain craves. We remember that which is most emotionally laden.

The amygdala, the brain's center for perception and processing of emotion, routes information to the prefrontal cortex. Emotions give us a more activated and chemically stimulated brain; they help us recall things

---

30. LeDoux, "Emotion, Memory, and Brain," 62.

31. Cohen, *Mature Mind*, 16.

better and form more explicit memories. The more intense the arousal of the amygdala, the stronger the memory imprint.[32]

Anticipation and curiosity create a positive state of hope and vigilance. This state causes increases in the activity of the attentional areas of the brain. Curiosity and anticipation are known as "appetitive" states because they stimulate the mental appetite.[33]

Good teachers capitalize on this state often. They know that it's the anticipation of positive events that drives up pleasure in the brain (dopamine) even more than the reward itself.[34]

Effective teachers engage emotion as part of the learning, not as an add-on. Some appropriate ways to include emotions in the classroom are

- compelling questions;

- role modeling;

- celebrations;

- physical activity;

- engineered controversy;

- purposeful physical rituals; and

- appealing to personal interests.

By continuing to learn and have new experiences, we can actively maintain, build, and remodel our brains for more effective and creative tasks. Doing so involves avoiding certain things as well.

Stress, excessive alcohol and drug use, inactivity, smoking, obesity, malnourishment, and social isolation all weaken the brain's neural superstructure. Prolonged stress seems to dramatically suppress new neuron production. Unrelenting stress kills neurons in the memory-rich hippocampus. There is no stable baseline for stress. Unlike other systems of the body that revert to a prior, healthy state, the brain responds to stress by developing a new, less healthy baseline. The Scriptures warn us about unhealthy practices. "Do you not know that you are the temple of God and that the Spirit of God dwells in you? If anyone defiles the temple of God,

---

32. Cahill, "Andrenergic," 702–4.

33. Bradley and Lang, "Measuring Emotion," 242–76. Cited in Jensen, *Teaching with Brain*, 77.

34. Schultz, "Neural Substrate," 1593.

God will destroy him. For the temple of God is holy, which temple you are" (1 Corinthians 3:16, 17 NKJV).

When students are in a state of excessive stress, fear, or anxiety, new information coming through the sensory intake areas of the brain cannot pass through the amygdala (temporal lobe) to gain access to the memory circuits. During high stress, new learning does not get into the information processing centers of the brain.

A school community of respect can be modeled, valued, and consistently reinforced. One way to build community is to incorporate specific stress-reducing and community-building strategies into classroom learning. Explicitly teach students how to reduce stress, control impulses, delay gratification, express feelings, and be a proactive friend.

> Before information can reach the relational, patterning, and memory storage areas of the brain, it must pass through the reticular activating system (RAS). If students associate their classrooms with visceral sense of fear, the RAS will filter out all but life-sustaining sensory information. This survival response to the stress of the classroom will greatly limit brain access to incoming information.[35]

> Several indicators can clue teachers into excessive student stress. For example, students may broadcast the stress of confusion by looking bored or acting out. Shortened attention spans are the brain's way of shutting out anxiety-producing confusion about material that is not being presented in an engaging and/or comprehensible manner.[36]

During times of mild to moderate stimulating challenges and positive emotion (contentment, joy, and comfortable conditions), there is a better working memory, improved verbal fluency, better episodic memory, and more flexible thinking yielding creative ideas for problem solving.

Whitman and Kelleher noted some known factors that cause and reduce stress. Factors that cause stress and lead to reactive brain flight, fight, or freeze responses are

- boredom,
- lack of personal relevance,

---

35. Cooper, Bloom, and Roth, *Biochemical Basis*; cited in Willis, *Brain-Friendly Strategies*, 44.

36. Meece, "Predictor of Math Anxiety," 69.

- frustration from previous failures,
- fear of being wrong in front of peers,
- fear of oral presentations,
- test-taking anxiety,
- physical differences or differences in language or dress,
- and being overwhelmed by the workload.

Factors that reduce stress and lead to the thinking, reflective brain responses are

- choice,
- novelty,
- humor,
- music,
- stories,
- anecdotes,
- kindness,
- movement,
- optimism,
- expressing gratitude,
- making predictions,
- and achieving challenges.[37]

When interest is high, stress and anxiety are decreased; and students are more accepting of their errors, more willing to try again, and less self-conscious about asking questions. Teachers have the capacity to fine-tune the level of stimulation versus stress in the classroom to achieve the right balance that inspires positive brain response and avoids stressors that impair brain efficiency and effective behavior.

---

37. Whitman and Kelleher, *Neuroteach*, 2016, 69.

Curriculum, Instruction, Assessments, and Learning

Knowing how the brain processes information and makes memories, and the content and curriculum chosen by teachers, profoundly impacts students' learning. There are several important questions to consider when selecting content for students to learn:

- Is it developmentally age-appropriate for the maturity of brain development?

- Is there an inclusion of big ideas with a focus on understanding?

- Is there enough flexibility to meet the needs of varying abilities and maturity of students?

- Does the content have any real-world connection?

- Does the curriculum cultivate a biblical worldview in students?

- Does this unit of instruction include time for students to learn how to manage time, study, organize, make judgments and decisions, and prioritize?

Classroom instructional practices can either motivate or demotivate students during the learning process. Some instructional practices enhance learning while others decrease the chance for long-term memory. Consider these important questions for improving long-term memory:

- Are students learning to learn, along with acquiring the necessary knowledge and skills?

- Are strategies used to stimulate the brain in multiple regions to enhance the chances of long-term memory?

The brain is poor at nonstop attention and needs time for processing and rest after learning. Refer to the suggested teacher guidelines on how long student attention typically lasts by age groups.

Guidelines for Direct Instruction of New Content

K-2	5–8 minutes
Grades 3–5	8–12 minutes
Grades 6–8	12–15 minutes
Grades 9–12	12–15 minutes
Adult Learners	15–18 minutes

Eric Jensen, *Teaching with the Brain in Mind*, p. 37

Planning major units that include authentic assessments (performance tasks) contributes to building memory dendrites. Authentic assessments require components of executive function, particularly higher conceptual thinking. These are some strategies for using authentic assessments:

- Discuss with students the expectations of the assessment.

- Provide students with a rubric that specifies the expectations early in the unit. Rubrics are like blueprints to guide executive function for students so they can plan, prioritize, monitor, and adjust their focus.

- Give students an opportunity to discuss or otherwise express their expectations of what a good teacher does when assessing students.

- Provide students with exemplars of student work.

Fear and Spiritual Development

Persistent fear inhibits the brain's ability to process information and learn. In addition, irrational fears and misconceptions keep us from becoming what God want us to be. Gaining knowledge about God's principles and how faith works is important because this can help rewire the brain so that fears do not control an individual's life. When an individual understands that God both cares about each person's day-to-day life experiences and orchestrates events on behalf of each individual, that knowledge reduces stress. The brain's built-in survival instincts are fulfilled by exercising faith based on God's good intentions for those he loves.

> For God hath not given us the spirit of fear; but of power,
> and of love, and of a sound mind.
>
> —2 TIMOTHY 1:7 NKJV

> Do not conform to the pattern of this world,
> but be transformed by the renewing of your mind.
>
> —ROMANS 12:2 NIV

Following Christ does not reduce circumstantial uncertainty, but it does reduce spiritual uncertainty. Faith gives us the courage to face circumstantial uncertainty. The goal in stressful situations is not to eliminate fear but to muster enough faith and courage to face and conquer our fears.[38]

Faith is unlearning the senseless worries and misguided beliefs that keep people captive. It is far more complex than simply modifying behavior. Faith rewires the brain. Neurologically, this is what happens when people study Scripture. Individuals are literally upgrading their minds by downloading the mind of Christ.

> Faith isn't about "playing it safe," but about choices
> that are calculated risks on the character and promises of God.
>
> —GARY INRIG

Key Chapter Takeaways

✓ Current brain research has revealed many things about how the brain learns that need to be put into practice in classrooms.

✓ Better understanding how memory works in the human brain helps educators better make use of it in their instructional planning.

---

38. Batterson, *In a Pit*, 44.

✓ Expert learners organize their knowledge around bigger ideas and concepts.

✓ There is no single, all-purpose resting location for all memories. Our best learning and recall involves multiple memory locations and systems. Thus, for optimal learning, teachers need to use a combination of instructional models (direct instruction, facilitating, and coaching) over the course of a unit.

✓ Brain rests and sleep allow the brain to recharge and transfer information from short-term to long-term memory.

✓ Physical activity, emotions, and stress all play roles in the brain's capacity to learn.

Concluding Thoughts

Judy Willis, neurologist and middle school classroom teacher, has the unique ability to see and understand the two worlds of neurology and K–12 curriculum, instruction, and assessment practices. She has written that it is unfortunate today that many schools are reacting to the current era of accountability with factory-style test prep instruction. She feels teachers are pressured to produce students whose standardized test scores will maintain their schools' rating and funding.[39] Because these tests are predominately a measure of rote learning rather than critical thinking, the curriculum can easily become dominated by rote instruction. Many teachers are following formulas in pursuit of higher test scores. This is frustrating during this time when brain-compatible teaching strategies to increase authentic, long-term learning are coming to light.

The new research into the brain is helping us better understand curriculum, discipline policies, assessment challenges, special education students, cafeteria food, the role of the arts, retention policies, and countless other aspects of the teaching profession. This is an exciting time!

—ERIC JENSON, TEACHING WITH THE BRAIN IN MIND

39. Willis, *Ignite*, 104.

So how do Christian schools respond to this current era of test prep accountability? Does the school's instructional program just focus on the basic knowledge and skills called for by today's standards? Is the school's mission the driving force behind all major decisions affecting the instructional program?

Incorporating these brain-based ideas into a school's instructional program could aid students in developing the necessary character, thinking ability, knowledge, and skills to be productive in God's kingdom in the twenty-first century.

The succeeding chapters delve into these questions more deeply.

Educator Interview

Q: How has research about how the brain best learns impacted you as an educator?

A: When I first began learning about brain research, I was so excited! What psychologists were discovering was *fascinating* to me. I knew we are fearfully and wonderfully made (Psalm 139:14), and the research was showing so much more of God's creation than I had ever imagined. I used my summers to research and learn new ways of teaching. It made sense because it was the way I myself best learned.

Elementary Principal

JEANNE NORTNESS

Bio

Teacher
Counselor
Christian School Principal

BA, Physical Education and Health, Central Washington University
MA, Curriculum and Instruction
Educational Technology
Leadership, Concordia Univeristy

I was first introduced to Understanding by Design around the year 2000. After trying it in my class of fourth graders, I experienced the excitement generated in students by using essential questions and authentic assessments.

Over the next five years, I was convicted in my teaching shortfalls. I remember praying, "Lord, please forgive my errors in past years of teaching. Don't let my mistakes keep my former students from loving to learn." Through my own research I learned better ways of engaging students, grading so students would be inspired to really learn, not just check an assignment off the list. I did away with punitive grading policies and tried assessing by using real-world situations. I had been teaching the way I was taught instead of teaching in ways students could learn better and enjoy learning.

Realizing students could only learn in small segments, I began teaching with shorter periods of instruction interleaved with times of processing and movement. I also integrated art and creative expressions more often. I started using strategies to up the engagement factor anywhere I could find them, and I began using visual teaching methods and challenges. I used some of the strategies in my own life because they worked, and I taught students to use them as well.

Q: **What specific things from brain research and cognitive psychology have especially affected your approach to education in a Christian elementary school environment that seeks to prepare students to "impact the world for Christ?"**

A: If students are going to make an impact for Christ, they must be full of God's love. In our school, we strive to make connections with all students. People often talk about the value of relationships in teaching, and a previous principal used to often remind us, "Remember, the important thing with kids is *relationship, relationship, relationship.*" The brain research agrees with this.

One of the most important things I have learned through the brain research and cognitive psychology is the fact students cannot learn when they are afraid. When I was in school, teachers were the bosses. What they said had better be followed, and I do not remember many teachers who showed warmth and care. Unfortunately, I was a product of my upbringing. I shudder to think of the way I talked to students when I first began teaching. I hate to admit it, but I would use belittling, sarcasm, and anger. So many times I have asked God to please work in my past students' lives despite my failures to help them thrive in a calm, respectful, and peaceful atmosphere.

Today, I often have opportunity to visit with students in disciplinary situations. The knowledge that nothing good will take place if either of us is in a heightened sense of emotion (anger, hurt, frustration, etc.) gives me great pause. Knowing the necessity of emotional and physical safety has made a difference in the way I listen, ponder, and try to help students solve their own problems.

Q: **As a Christian school principal, how has your staff reacted to the knowledge about learning from current brain research and cognitive psychology?**

A: Our teachers are eagerly learning to incorporate current brain research ideas into their teaching, partially because teachers are learners and partially because Christian teachers, especially, have a deep desire to do the absolute best for their students. I've noticed teachers gradually incorporating teaching strategies shown to make a difference in learning.

Nearly all, if not all, our teachers emphasize a growth mind-set with students. Walking through classrooms, I often hear the encouraging "You can't do it yet" when responding to the often-heard "I can't do it!" Teachers not only encourage students to have a growth mindset, but they are also experiencing it for themselves.

The COVID-19 season with teachers teaching remotely spurred our staff to learn how to do distant learning better and better, and they yearned to find out what others were doing. Teachers could have done the minimum, but even though some of the technology needed was outside their realm of understanding, they pushed ahead to learn and practice new ways of doing things. As many educational leaders would most likely agree, teachers went above and beyond to learn best practices for keeping relationships strong and helping students keep learning. They model a growth mindset.

Some of the strategies to help students learn and retain have been around for many years. For example, teaching by using multiple senses was not new to our teachers. Teachers understood the value of using images and various graphic organizers before I came into my position as an educational leader. I often see a KWL chart in classes to help students access previously learned content and relearn where misconceptions may exist. Other strategies help students make connections in their minds as well. I have seen teachers "make memories" by using food, memorable learning activities, music, and humor in their teaching. To a lesser degree, I see novel and unusual introductions and experiences. Our teachers show by their teaching they understand variety is the spice of life and of learning.

We are also learning the value of alternating between short input sessions and then taking time to process. Rare is the long, drawn-out lecture style of teaching.

As we as a staff keep growing in our own comprehension and use of Understanding by Design, I see a real thrill in teachers as they share the fun, excitement, and student engagement of a well-designed unit in UbD. It's like there is no turning back when teachers see this in a classroom. Using authentic assessments has been difficult at first, but teachers are finding it easier and easier, just like anything that is hard at first. More importantly, though, students find classes more fun yet challenging, and they seem to put more effort into "real-life" situations.

PHYSICAL ACTIVITY

I love the quote by Morton Blackwell: "The mind can absorb no more than the seat can endure." Our teachers are beginning to understand the value of movement breaks during class and recess. Processing time for students is often up, out of their seats, and moving around the room. They make use of a "gallery walk" type of activity or maybe get up and talk to a partner across the room. Kids have the chance to get up out of their seats, get the blood circulating in their legs, see different scenery, and dialogue in order to help cement new learning. Teachers with clear expectations find no loss of time teaching when using this strategy. Socialization is strengthened with a communication target, and pathways in the brain are built up. The movement gives students a chance to come back ready to listen and be more productive.

In previous years, recesses were often taken from students for various reasons. We are learning the real value of recess. Teachers use the loss of recess less and less often as a disciplinary measure because they understand the need to move, socialize, and take a break from the classroom routine. In our area of the country, we often have inside recesses. Teachers have many options for students when we have an inside recess day; students have choice in what they do—some needing and choosing more physical activity than others.

EMOTIONS, STRESS, AND ANXIETY

I am so proud of our teachers. They get it. They are learning that students cannot learn when their fearful emotions are heightened. Teachers are making it okay for students to take a break when they are feeling unsafe because an assignment is just more than they can handle or social problems are overwhelming at the time. Some students have a hard time learning because their family is torn apart, and they have their own emotional struggles. Teachers are making a safe classroom and making allowances for emotional flare-ups. Many teachers have some type of gathering time each day when students can share needs and prayer requests and encourage each other.

INSTRUCTIONAL DESIGN

Moving to Understanding by Design has been one of the most exciting developments in our school over the past few years. We are starting to see progress in this new way of doing school, but we still have more to learn and incorporate. Teachers are less tied to published curriculum as they plan units with their goals for students in mind. Teachers are seeing the value of enduring understandings, and they can almost see the gears moving in students as students struggle to think deeper about big ideas. Of course, this change is not easy. We all are pretty used to the status quo, and students would rather give the quick answer instead of thinking deeply. However, we are starting to see more and more evidence of students working hard, tackling challenges, and making connections in their brains and learnings.

Q: **Your school has made significant changes in its instructional program based on current brain research. What have been some of the most rewarding changes? What have been some of the greatest challenges?**

A: Our school is in the process of making a significant turn in our instructional program. Three Rivers Christian School is becoming an Understanding by Design school. We have been in this transition for about three years now, and some exciting changes have occurred and there are some more on the horizon. We were advised at the beginning of this process to expect three to five years to see maximum results, so I guess we are about on track. How is it going? In all honesty, we see some exciting changes as well as some challenges.

One of the exciting aspects of this transition is to see and hear a teacher who after going through the challenge of putting together a well-designed Understanding by Design unit is feeling the thrill of victory—victory in seeing students having fun learning and showing their own excitement over learning. Assessments coming out of these units have the right amount of challenge balanced with the necessary supports. This "just right" investigation results in students engaged and striving without feeling overwhelmed. Students love doing work that has real-world context, and teachers seem to enjoy teaching this way.

Another shift I have seen has to do with grading practices. I have noticed teachers moving away from zeros in the gradebook toward grace in grading. We are in the process of moving to a totally different reporting system in which parents and students get a better picture of the total child. Grading is not so much of a "gotcha" in order to reward or punish a student for behavior but more of an encouragement. Our teachers give better feedback and accept revisions. Students get the message, "You are still learning. You can try it again, and the better score will count."

I also see a shift away from simply learning facts. Oh, we know facts and skills are necessary, but the focus now is using the facts and skills to make sense of things. Teachers are much less likely to use timed tests instead of assessments to give students a chance to show they really "get it." Of course, many parents don't understand this move. As we communicate with parents why we do what we do, they sometimes nod and accept it, but just as this process is taking time for teachers, it also will take time for parents. After all, they were not taught this way.

Finally, focusing on big ideas and enduring understandings is helping us clear out some of the content in our curriculum that is maybe helpful, but not absolutely necessary. As any teacher using published curriculum knows it's just too much! Our school is narrowing the breadth of curriculum while trying to go deeper with greater mastery.

We are growing and improving, all of which is so rewarding. Is it tough? Yes. Do we have challenges? Of course. One of our greatest challenges is probably common to most schools transitioning their instructional program—time. Our teachers are amazing! However, amazing comes because they pour themselves into their work and ministry. As a result, some teachers take a little longer to really buy in to the new ways of educating students. Good things are happening, yet it takes time to feel comfortable going a different direction. I am confident, though, our staff will all get there. The early adopters do bring a great deal of encouragement, but even those who take time to observe, analyze, and find what works best are valuable members of the organization. We are each a part of the TRCS body, and the body grows and builds itself up in love as each one does one's part (see Ephesians 4:16).

Q: What advice would you give to other Christian school administrators who desire to make significant changes in their school's instructional program based on current brain research and cognitive psychology information?

A: My advice to other Christian school administrators and teachers who want to improve their instructional program based on current brain research is to take a deep dive into Understanding by Design. Although UbD has been around for over twenty years, I have noticed in recent years that it is coming to the forefront of instructional design. Read the books about UbD. Attend Jay McTighe's workshop if possible. Check it out completely, because adapting UbD is a systemic change, and you want to know it is good.

One of the best things we did in pursuing Understanding by Design is to utilize a good consultant who has pushed us to learn, to struggle, and to refine our total program. Someone from outside your own organization can see things from a different perspective. We would not be where we are today without this help.

Educator Interview

Q: How has research about how the brain best learns impacted you as an educator?

A: What I now know about the brain and how it works has really impacted me as an educator. I am now very intentional about creating variety in my learning opportunities. I'd always done this, but I now focus on doing it more often. I understand the length of time a student can focus on learning is directly related to age, brain development, and the quality of my lesson. I must frequently vary my teaching techniques, student interaction, and learning opportunities to create deeper understanding. The understanding of how and when the brain develops has also helped me to decide what types of activities to use for certain age groups.

Secondary School Principal

BRICE RICHARDS

Bio

Public School Teacher
Christian School Secondary
  Principal

BA, Central Washington University
MBA, Washington State University
MAT, City University
National Board Certified Teacher:
  Early Adolescence Mathematics

Q: Are there specific things from brain research and cognitive psychology that have especially affected your approach to education for teenagers in a Christian environment that seeks to prepare students to "impact the world for Christ?"

A: The teenage mind is something completely fascinating. The amount of knowledge a teen student can learn in a given time is amazing. I have also been impressed with the level of critical thinking and deep understanding a teenage student can demonstrate. What is amusing is also how little processing is used at times. I have come to understand when a teen says, "I don't know why I did _____," they honestly mean it! We have to keep in mind these are young adults capable of amazing things, and we can't underestimate their abilities. On the other hand, we must give them space to make mistakes. We know they will act impulsively or not think things through at times. Let's use those times as opportunities to learn from. Learning from a mistake will create lasting understanding for sure.

Q: As a Christian secondary school principal, how has your staff reacted to the knowledge about learning from current brain research and cognitive psychology?

A: My staff has embraced the learning about brain research in many ways. I have seen them consider a much more holistic approach to educating the student. We are very interested in not only how the student is doing academically but how they are developing in life. We genuinely care for our students, and this research has allowed us to understand how to support them better. We really take the time to watch for emotional stress, fatigue, the need for extensions or interventions, and much more.

A big area of focus for us this year (which turned out to be a good choice with the home quarantine from COVID-19) was teacher and student stress. We really spent some time studying how students' stress was impacting their ability to learn. We tried to provide a number of ways to help accommodate learning needs to achieve great results, but also do it in a supported stress environment. Another revelation to us that we hadn't been aware of before was the amount of stress a teacher demonstrated and how it impacted their students. We are all human and have bad days or have stress from outside of work. We do a great job of masking our stress at times, but studies have shown when our cortisol levels are high, the students' levels will also rise. The rise in cortisol lowers their ability to learn. Our teachers focused a lot this year on positive stress management techniques of their own, from sleep habits to building more supportive relationships.

Q: You have a unique perspective of Christian schools because of your background of serving in Christian schools and public schools. What similarities and differences have you seen that brain research and cognitive psychology have had in these two environments?

A: I believe there are similarities and differences between public school and Christian education. Overall, I think they both intend to create adults who will impact the world as functional members of society. I think both models were created out of ideals around doing what is best for the students. However, I think the public school model is broken with regards to the measure of success.

I can't speak for all public schools, but I know I feel the system I've experienced is broken. I don't think high-stakes testing and evaluation of student future success solely on a letter grade is adequate. In this system, we aren't valuing the development of all learning interests. I know I used to think I was, but as I taught longer and longer in public school, I felt restricted by the constraint of pushing for year-end test results. This push went against my heart's passion of creating students who believed in themselves, worked to the best of their abilities, and realized they were born with special skills and gifts. Maybe the subject they were in was challenging for them or it was one they loved, but either way they could be great at it. I wanted to foster a passion for lifelong learning, and a desire to impact the world.

In Christian school, I can help students understand they were born with a purpose, with learning aptitudes, and have developed interests God was going to bring together and use them to impact the world for him. I feel public school has become how I can achieve the next step—the *A*, college, then work for forty years. Who made this the definition of success? I believe serving our God and loving others to the best of our abilities is a lofty goal we can all work toward and achieve. I have learned much in my life through my Christian walk. One main thing is no matter what grades I achieved, what degrees I accumulated, what jobs I had, and what pay I received, there was never anything more satisfying than loving the Lord and serving others. That is the difference for me in the two models. I personally feel more freedom to do the latter in the Christian school setting.

Q: **What advice would you give to other Christian school administrators who are desiring to make significant changes in their Christian school's instructional program based on current brain research and cognitive psychology ideas?**

A: Generally, I think the current push in "school culture" is to be less relational. We have a generation with the most social connectivity ever with technology. Yet studies show students feel the least connected. I see this as detrimental for students, impacting how they feel about themselves. Brain research and Scripture show us we need positive supportive relationships in our lives. This fellowship helps to form a positive self-perspective in our students. When we love the Lord and love others, we create a sustainable, supportive learning environment where students can come to learn and feel supported in doing so.

3

Mission-Focused Instructional Design

> There is a difference between a Christian teacher
> and teacher who is Christian.
>
> —ROY LOWRIE,
> *To Those Who Teach in Christian Schools*

AT THE HEART OF any Christian school is the staff. The Christian school administrators and teachers see the spiritual dimension in education and represent Christ in their schools and classrooms. As Roy Lowrie writes, they have a

- clear testimony of Christ being their Savior and are able to convey the importance of this to their students;

- strong sense of God's leading into teaching (teaching in a Christian school is not just a job);

- strong sense of God's leading them to this particular school; and

- close walk with God including study of the Scriptures and prayerful personal devotions.[1]

With this foundation, Christian school staff undertake the essential task of crafting the instructional program of their Christian school.

1. List summarized from Lowrie, *Those Who Teach*, 3–5.

45

Educational researcher Robert Marzano has concluded that a "guaranteed and viable curriculum is the number-one school-level factor impacting student achievement."[2] If the curriculum makes that much difference in student engagement, development, and performance, it then behooves a school's staff to dedicate a considerable amount of effort in deciding what should be taught, how it should be taught, and how it will be assessed. These three elements—curriculum, instruction, and assessment—are the foundations of quality instructional design.

Teachers often do not think about it, but they are designers. High-quality instructional design is an essential skill for teachers. In reality, nominal attention is given to instructional design in teacher education programs or in the ongoing staff development that administrators and teachers participate in during their careers.

Units of instruction and individual lessons are at times quickly put together and habitually taught with little revision or peer review for improvement. Some teachers take the time to review student results through item analysis of the summary test at the end of a unit, but rarely is sufficient time committed by staff to first develop curriculum and lessons, then review units of instruction and analyze the student work.

Flawed Instructional Design

The two most common curriculum approaches used in schools are activity-based lessons and coverage lessons. Today, the content is driven by standards that have unreasonable amounts of content and usually focus on only basic knowledge and skills.

Activity-based lessons are more typically used at the elementary levels and are fun and engaging but are often without clear purpose, as they are not aligned to outcomes or content and performance standards.

Coverage lessons are usually designed to march through textbooks or course outlines with no overarching ideas or transfer objectives. Jerome Bruner delineated three reasons traditional coverage of content is uneconomical in the long run:

1. Such teaching makes it difficult for the student to generalize from what he has learned to what he will encounter later.

2. Such learning has little reward in terms of intellectual excitement.

2. Marzano, *What Works*, 22.

3. Knowledge one has acquired without sufficient structure to tie it together is knowledge that is likely to be forgotten. An unconnected set of facts has a pitiably short half-life in memory.[3]

In traditional academic curriculum design, the learners' need to try to apply their learning in genuine situations is most often not included because of the pressure of too much content to cover. Even though brain research reveals that retention is clearly better when application is used in the learning process, there is still a propensity to cover lots of content with little application and transfer.

Improving Instructional Design

Based on current brain research, views on effective learning have shifted from just diligent drill and practice to a focus on students' understanding and application of knowledge. Learning must be guided by generalized principles in order to be widely applicable. As discussed in the previous chapter, knowledge learned at the level of rote memory rarely transfers.

Experts first seek to develop understanding of problems, and this often involves thinking in terms of core concepts or big ideas. Novice learners generally approach problems by searching for correct formulas and pat answers.

Research on developing expertise suggests that superficial coverage of many topics in the domain may be a poor way to help students develop the competencies that will prepare them for future learning and work. In addition, many assessments measure only factual knowledge.

The single greatest determinant of learning is not socioeconomic factors or funding levels. It is instruction.

—MIKE SCHMOKER

Christian school educational professionals should be most interested in the results (what students have learned) and what works to get the results that their mission has specified. The academic freedom that teachers have should be guided by research-based learning principles and best practices in

---

3. Bruner, *Process of Education*, 31.

the profession. Knowing that there is too much content, and understanding high-quality instructional design practices, help guide curricular choices.

Expert teachers know the structure of their disciplines, and this provides them with cognitive roadmaps that guide the assignments they give students, the assessments they use to gauge student progress, and the questions they ask.

Expert teachers know:

- the cognitive roadmaps of content;

- that superficial coverage of many topics is not very productive;

- that students' understanding and application of knowledge is more fruitful than just drill and practice;

- that expert learners organize discrete ideas around core concepts and generalized principles rather than depending on just rote memory;

- that novice learners look for correct formulas and pat answers; and

- that constructive feedback (formative assessment) is scarce in classrooms.[4]

Exceptional learners also use the strategy of metacognition—thinking about your thinking. These students are mindful of how they learn, set personal goals, regularly self-assess and adjust their performance, and use productive strategies to assist their learning. Less effective learners are usually clueless about their preferred learning style and strategies to improve their learning, don't set goals, and rarely self-assess. Research and experience have shown that metacognitive strategies can be taught, and less capable learners can greatly benefit from using these strategies.

Focusing on the Mission

David I. Smith argues in his book *On Christian Teaching: Practicing Faith in the Classroom* that there is persistently a gap between Christian statements of educational mission and daily realities of educational practice. So where does a school start on this process of improving instructional design processes? What should be the focus? In many schools, it is left up to each teacher to determine what is important to be taught.

---

4. Bransford, *How People Learn*, 155–56.

One effective approach is to use the school's mission statement to provide direction. A school's mission statement reveals which particular purpose(s) are most important. Schools teach many different things, but concentrating on a few key mission-related purposes provides a common emphasis for staff to strive toward in the design of the educational program.

There are a variety of ways to construct mission statements. Some schools' mission statements clearly call out distinct purposes and/or attributes while others are more general. In the latter instance, staff will need to take the time to ferret out the purposes and attributes that are the school's highest priorities. This is not a difficult task. It requires giving staff some time to brainstorm their primary outcome goals, to prioritize them, and to finally refine the results.

Regardless of the process, once schools have developed a clear picture of the outcomes most desired (e.g., students will have developed godly character), and defined what this will look like by specific indicators (e.g., they are individuals who demonstrate integrity, responsibility, and perseverance as productive members of society), then working on curriculum, instruction, and assessment practices with these as priority becomes well-focused. When discussions occur about content coverage over the course of a K–8 or K–12 Christian school program, the question "Where does the mission play out in the day-to-day instruction?" becomes easier to plan for and assess. Collecting evidence that a school is achieving its mission also becomes attainable. There will be more discussion about this in succeeding chapters, "Assessing for What Is Most Important" (Chapter 4) and "Systemic Thinking" (Chapter 6).

Following are two typical examples of mission statements from Christian schools, one whose mission is very specific and the other that is not. Each school has fleshed out its most important indicators of its mission with concrete markers.

Grace Cascade Christian Schools

Grace Cascade Christian Schools exist as a faithful instrument in God's hands to assist Christian families by providing a biblically based education designed to cultivate spiritual maturity, godly character, strong scholarship, and selfless service to others, resulting in students who know Jesus Christ personally and make him known.

Portrait of a Graduate

SPIRITUAL MATURITY

- Views the Scriptures as inerrant and relevant and daily reads the Holy Bible
- Relies on Scripture to formulate a worldview
- Spends time in prayer, alone and/or with others, each day
- Strives to honor the Lord in all that they say, think, and do

GODLY CHARACTER

- Understands the redemption we have in Christ and seeks to reflect that redemption through unwavering trust in the sovereignty of God (even in the face of trial)
- Forgives easily (quick to listen, slow to speak, slow to become angry)
- Treats others with empathy and kindness, honoring each person's differences and uniqueness as image bearers of God
- Is generous and grateful

STRONG SCHOLARSHIP

- Possesses a lifelong love of learning
- Consistently puts forth their best effort in all that they do academically
- Refrains from cheating in any form, from giving or receiving unacknowledged aid to plagiarism
- Is able to collaborate with peers and nonpeers to research, create, and present ideas, concepts, findings, and projects.
- Possesses strong and effective oral, written, and presentation communication skills

SELFLESS SERVICE

- Serves as a mentor to peers or an underclassman
- Humbly serves others without desire to be noticed or recognized, always deferring glory to God
- Works cheerfully, with a good attitude
- Serves as a peacemaker, reconciling people to God and others

KNOWS CHRIST

- Knows, loves, submits to, and shares Christ
- Knows Christ and is committed to making him known
- Manifests love, joy, peace, patience, kindness, goodness, faithfulness, gentleness, self-control
- Understands role as a steward, not an owner

MAKES CHRIST KNOWN

- Knows how to use the Bible to explain the gospel of Christ
- Will display without words the character Christ has set forth for his followers
- Treats everyone as an image bearer of God
- Sees a need and quietly meets the need as an ambassador for Christ in the community

Three Rivers Christian School Mission

The mission of Three Rivers Christian School is to prepare students from infancy through twelfth grade to impact the world for Christ.

Graduate Attributes

Students will be *servant leaders* who give "feet to their faith," living out the Greatest Commandment in both thought and action, loving and serving others compassionately after Christ's example. They are individuals who

- have accepted and follow Jesus Christ as their Lord and Savior, developed a respect and love for the Bible, and understand that the Scriptures are God's truth to mankind;

- are contributing members of their communities who are willing to serve others;

- engage regularly in leadership opportunities with a problem-solving outlook;

- demonstrate integrity, responsibility, and perseverance as productive members of community;

- understand the value of and are responsible to use material and knowledge resources for the glory of God; and

- understand the importance of the church and are committed to evangelism.

Students will be *perseverant*, who understand the value of grit and determination in developing their own ability and gifts and relentlessly pursuing growth. They are individuals who

- manage projects with persistence, even in the face of opposition, and value time as a God-given commodity;

- value learning as one of God's privileges and appreciate and love learning;

- are curious and are responsible for their own learning and actions;

- take initiative and work independently, which results in bringing honor to the Lord; and

- read and comprehend a variety of materials.

Students will be *capable communicators* who are prepared to participate in community through winsome and clear communication. They are individuals who

- demonstrate the principles of effective and godly communication;

- are able to work collaboratively face-to-face, in writing, or through electronic media situations;

- articulately, effectively, and persuasively communicate orally, in writing, and artistically to a range of audiences in a variety of ways; and

- are accountable for their actions, treat everyone with respect, see issues from different perspectives because all are made in God's image.

Students will be *relational* and will seek to understand and value the individual gifts of themselves and others and see themselves in the collaborative context of their community and the world that they will impact. They are individuals who

- understand the importance of biblical ethics and actions in relationships;

- are kind-hearted, sociable, and friendly;

- listen with understanding and empathy, follow instructions, and request clarification;

- understand they are uniquely created by God and continue to grow in character;

- show respect for and submission to God, family, and all other authority; and

- have respect for our Christian and American heritage.

Students will be *discerning thinkers* who will be prepared to encounter the world and its philosophies and interpret society's changing thoughts with a solid framework of wisdom grounded in Jesus. They are individuals who

- are reflective and depend on God for wisdom based on biblical standards and truths;

- reason logically, looking for truth and using evidence for critical analysis;

- are patient and seek to understand complex situations, giving consideration to different points of view;

- use diverse strategies and a biblical perspective in solving problems, making decisions, evaluating results, and applying knowledge to real-life situations; and

- are creative and use critical thinking skills.

Tools for Improving Instructional Design

There are two basic curriculum models: traditional and backward design. The conventional traditional lesson design model is to plan a series of lessons on a topic, creating a related assessment toward the end of the teaching on this topic. This consumption model is characterized by

- being topic-driven;

- focusing on recall;

- having control of isolated elements as the goal; and

- being linear: a march of coverage.

Using the backward lesson design model, teachers first identify the desired learning results and determine acceptable evidence, then plan the instruction and learning experiences. It is characterized by

- being results-driven;

- focusing on understanding;

- emphasizing transfer to new situations; and

- being recursive—big ideas and transfer tasks continually recur.

As noted earlier, the conventional approach is the norm in most schools, including Christian schools. The backward design approach was first purported by Ralph Tyler in 1949 when he described the logic of backward design clearly and succinctly. Today, Jay McTighe and the late Grant Wiggins have operationalized backward design principles, calling the framework "Understanding by Design." Their first publication, *Understanding by Design*, appeared in 1998.[5]

5. Both Wiggins and McTighe bring a wealth of experience developed during rich and varied careers in education. Jay McTighe is an accomplished author, having co-authored fourteen books, including the award-winning and best-selling *Understanding by Design* series with Grant Wiggins. His books have been translated into ten languages. He has also written more than thirty-five articles and book chapters, and has been published in leading

"What is perhaps new is what we offer: a process and set of tools (templates and filters) to make the selection of curriculum priorities more likely to happen by design than by good fortune."[6] The principle of backward design of curriculum is straightforward—begin with the end in mind and design toward it. The primary value of backward design is its ability to encourage educators to design instruction that gets at the core ideas and questions that form the basis of the discipline or subject they teach.

Teachers start with the end (the desired results) and then identify the evidence necessary to determine that the results have been achieved (assessments). With the results and assessments clearly specified, educators determine the necessary (enabling) knowledge and skills and, only then, the teaching needed to equip students to perform.

Understanding by Design (UbD) is not a prescriptive program, an instructional model, or incompatible with some subject areas. The UbD framework can be used by teachers in kindergarten and by professors in graduate school. Understanding by Design does provide a framework for planning, promotes a way of thinking, and encourages quality control through a set of design standards.

Understanding by Design

In one of his recent books, *Upgrade Your Teaching: Understanding by Design Meets Neuroscience*, Jay McTighe outlines seven key tenets of Understanding by Design:

1. Learning is enhanced when teachers *think purposefully* about curriculum planning. The UbD framework supports thoughtful curriculum design without offering a rigid process or prescriptive program.

2. The framework helps focus curriculum and teaching on *the development and deepening of student understanding and transfer of learning*—that is, the ability to effectively use content knowledge and skill.

3. Understanding is revealed when students can *make sense of and transfer their learning through authentic performance*. Six facets of understanding—the capacity to explain, interpret, apply, shift perspective, empathize, and self-assess—can serve as indicators of understanding.

---

journals, including *Educational Leadership* (ASCD) and *Education Week*.

6. Wiggins and McTighe, *Understanding by Design*, 12.

4. Effective *curriculum is planned backward from long-term outcomes* through a three-stage design process. This process helps avoid three common educational problems: (a) treating the textbook as the curriculum rather than a resource; (b) activity-oriented teaching in which no clear priorities and purposes are apparent; and (c) test prep, in which students practice the format of standardized tests (usually selected-response items) while concentrating on only tested content.

5. *Teachers are coaches of understanding*, not mere purveyors of content knowledge, skill, or activity. They focus on ensuring that transfer of learning happens, rather than just assuming that students learned what was taught.

6. Regular *reviews of curriculum against design standards* enhance curricular quality, leading to deeper learning; at the same time, concomitant reviews of student work in professional learning communities inform needed adjustments in curriculum and instruction so that student learning is maximized.

7. Teachers, schools, and districts can "work smarter" and more effectively by *sharing their curriculum designs with others.*[7]

Instruction in UbD-designed units focuses on understanding and transfer while providing opportunity for intentionally planned biblical integration, differentiation, technology integration, and metacognition activities.

In today's classroom, teachers feel the pressure to cover large amounts of content, often in conjunction with teaching a certain number of textbook chapters. In the Understanding by Design framework, the focus is on uncovering understandings. Uncoverage is required for understanding of the content and transfer. There are three types of uncoverage:

- uncovering core ideas at the heart of understanding

- uncovering questions, issues, assumptions, and gray areas

- uncovering potential student misunderstandings

The structure of knowledge is often viewed in three levels: knowledge and skills, key concepts and core processes, and principles and generalizations. Most educators are highly skilled at teaching facts and skills, as this has been the focus for many years. Understanding by Design provides

---

7. McTighe and Willis, *Upgrade Your Teaching*, 22–23.

teachers with ways to rethink units of instruction, including the key concepts and core processes and principles and generalizations.

The Understanding by Design framework is laid out in three steps:

Stage 1. Identify the desired learning results.

Stage 2. Determine the acceptable evidence.

Stage 3. Plan the learning experiences and instruction.

BACKWARD DESIGN MODEL

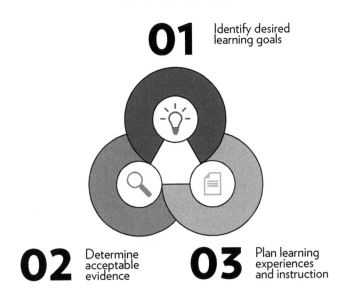

01 Identify desired learning goals

02 Determine acceptable evidence

03 Plan learning experiences and instruction

Based on data from Jay McTighe and Grant Wiggins, *Understanding by Design 2nd Edition,* ASCD, 2005 p. 18.

This book is not designed to give an in-depth explanation of each of the stages, but will give the reader an overview of the key elements and terms, and how a Christian school can use them to become more mission-focused. Wiggins and McTighe have written numerous books and articles about this planning framework that can be used to gain deeper understanding.[8]

8. The bibliography lists several of the key books, and most can be found at the ASCD website: www.ascd.org/books-publications.aspx.

In *Understanding by Design*, the desired learning results are delineated several ways: big ideas, enduring understandings, essential questions, knowledge, and skills. Teachers first select the big idea of their unit. Then they are asked to consider established goals and standards that should be included in the unit, along with deciding on specific enduring understandings and essential questions. Lastly, the essential knowledge and skills are identified that are necessary for achieving the desired learning results.

Because the backward design process is foreign to many Christian school educators, this process is awkward and challenging at first. Thinking in this manner takes time to develop but yields many positive benefits for students' understanding and ability to transfer what they have learned. In addition, teachers find greater satisfaction with their teaching, as it is very engaging for them and appeals to their interest in developing the whole student rather than just preparing students to pass standardized assessments.

Big Ideas

"We turn now to the questions of how experts' knowledge is organized . . . Their knowledge is not simply a list of facts and formulas that are relevant to the domain; instead, their knowledge is organized around core concepts or 'big ideas' that guide their thinking about the domain."[9]

Big ideas can be core concepts, overarching principles, organizing theories, underlying assumptions, focusing themes, processes, etc. that should serve as the focal point of curriculum, instruction, and assessment. Big ideas can be thought of as the meaningful patterns that enable us to "connect the dots" of otherwise fragmented knowledge. Big ideas often generate knowledge that can transfer into new and different contexts.

As noted in the chapter on brain research, expert learners naturally use big ideas to organize knowledge in their brains. So if the brain prefers this manner of organization, why shouldn't teachers use this fact to their advantage when designing units and lessons.

Wiggins and McTighe have developed several good questions for identifying a big idea:

- Does it reflect a core idea, as judged by experts?

- Does it have many layers and is not obvious to the naive or inexperienced learner?

9. Bransford et al., *How People Learn*, 24.

- Can it yield great power, depth, and breadth of insight into this subject?

- Do you have to dig deep to really understand its subtle meanings and implications, even though there is a surface understanding?

- Is it prone to misunderstanding as well as disagreement?

- Are you likely to change your mind about its meaning and importance over a lifetime?

Christian schools are ripe with opportunities to consider big ideas that have biblical implications in every content area, not just in Bible classes. Below are a few examples:

- In mathematics: God and infinity; complexity

- In science: creation vs. evolution; the intricacies of creation

- In social studies: God's history or man's history; the value of history; conflict; democracy vs. tyranny

- In English: man's condition and God's plan for man; the value of literature; literature and culture

- In world languages: universality of language

- In Bible: good vs. evil; wisdom; character

- In the arts: creativity; God's view of art, music, culture, and society

- In physical education: health and fitness; competition

- In technology: God and technology

Enduring Understandings

Enduring understandings are phrased in complete sentences, focus on big ideas, are abstract and transferable to other disciplines and periods of life, and/or require uncoverage and thought. When constructing enduring understandings, consider whether they

- represent a "big idea" that has enduring value beyond the classroom (transfer);

- reside at the heart or core of the discipline;

- require uncoverage; and

- engage students.

Understanding (the noun) involves more than just knowing information. It refers to the specific inferences, based on big ideas, that have lasting value beyond the classroom. When a student understands, they can make meaning of facts. In Understanding by Design, designers are encouraged to write them as full-sentence statements, describing what, specifically, students should understand about the topic. The stem "Students will understand that . . ." provides a practical tool for identifying enduring understandings.

"You can forget facts, but you cannot forget understanding."
—ERIC MAZUR, PHYSICIST AND EDUCATOR

Enduring understandings are not vague generalities. Instead, they are attainable specifics tailored to the abilities of the students. Example: *I want students to understand the Civil War.* At the elementary level, an appropriate goal might be *I want students to understand the causes of the Civil War.* Or at the secondary level, *I want students to understand that there were several significant and interrelated causes of the Civil War—the morality of slavery, fundamentally different views about the role of the federal government, dissimilarities of regional economies, and a clash of cultures.*

Essential Questions

Essential questions are doorways for exploring the big ideas that lead to the desired understandings. Essential questions are often used in the instructional process when units of instruction are initiated. Many teachers post the essential questions and periodically refer to them as the unit unfolds. They give students insight into the unit and allow thoughtful opportunities to occur where students can rethink their responses. Teachers can use essential questions as a basis for review and/or evaluation.

According to Grant Wiggins and Jay McTighe, qualities of essential questions are that they

- engage students in inquiry;
- have no right answer;
- spark lively discussion, sustained inquiry, and new understandings;
- improve students' skills;

- encourage students to rethink big ideas, assumptions, and prior learning;

- have meaningful connections to prior learning and personal experiences; and

- transfer to other subjects, eras, and situations.

Essential questions can be categorized in several ways:

- Philosophical: What is justice? Is art a matter of taste or principle? Should we clone life?

- Epistemological: Is history inevitably biased? Is mathematics discovery or invention?

- Making Meaning: In what ways does light act wavelike? Does separation of powers lead to gridlock? What do good readers do?

- Metacognitive/Reflective: What is working? What isn't? What adjustments do I need to make? What did I learn?

Teachers are masters at asking questions in the classroom. Most teacher questions are used to seek a right answer. Both shy students and students with less academic background are fearful to respond to these types of questions and seldom participate. These questions have their place in the classroom, but so do essential questions, as they allow for exploration of ideas. Teachers are often surprised by which students respond and how thoughtful they are when asked essential questions. They are often those reticent students.

Again, there are unlimited opportunities to use enduring understandings and essential questions for integration of biblical ideas into every content area. Following are several examples:

Mathematics

Big Idea: Complexity

Enduring Understanding: Students will understand that mathematics (infinity, probability, statistics, set theory, etc.) reveals the amazing complexity of the universe that God has created.

Essential Question: How do mathematical ideas (infinity, probability, statistics, set theory, etc.) reveal the complexity of creation?

Science

Big Idea: Creation vs. Evolution

Enduring Understanding: Students will understand that belief in creation takes less faith than the belief that the universe and life exist by chance.

Essential Questions: What takes more faith, creationism or evolution by chance? Are there key differences between creationism and evolution?

Social Studies

Big Idea: God's History or Man's History

Enduring Understandings: Students will understand that God's view of history is through the lens of salvation for mankind.
    Students will understand that the world's view of perspective is that "perception is reality."

Essential Questions: How do we know that our perspective of history is what God sees? What is the world's view of perspective?

English-Language Arts

Big Idea: The Value of Literature

Enduring Understandings: Students will understand that the best literature reveals our sinful human nature and points men to God for redemption. The world considers literature good when it articulately reveals man's nature.
    Students will understand that the Bible provides rich and timeless insights into the key themes, dilemmas, and challenges of mankind.

Essential Questions: How do we know that literature is good? What does the world hold as good literature? Why read the Bible as literature?

World Languages

Big Idea: Universality of Language

Enduring Understanding: Students will understand that, early in recorded history at the time of the Tower of Babel, God decided that multiple languages were necessary to keep mankind from depending on men's ingenuity, cleverness, or creativity (Genesis 11:1–9).

Essential Question: Is there a relationship between the many languages on earth and the difficulty in communication and sin?

Bible

Big Idea: Good vs. Evil

Enduring Understanding: Students will understand that the struggle between good and evil has existed from the earliest times in recorded human history.

Essential Question: Do good and evil actually exist?

The Arts

Big Idea: God's View of Art

Enduring Understanding: Students will understand that history as seen through the eyes of the artist is often a powerful and meaningful way to understand God's hand in history.

Essential Question: What role could a Christian artist play in society?

Physical Education

Big Idea: Health and Fitness

Enduring Understanding: Students will understand that God has created the body as the temple of the Holy Spirit, and he expects us to use our body for his honor (1 Corinthians 6:17).

Essential Question: Does God care about how we treat or use our bodies?

Technology

Big Idea: God and Technology

Enduring Understanding: Students will understand that throughout history technological advances have been used for good and evil (weapons for protection or national/personal gain at someone else's expense).

Essential Question: Is technology good or evil?

Open-ended questions cultivate reflection and encourage the respondent to consider their beliefs and motivations. It is interesting to note that God was the first to ask essential questions and still does so today when we are listening. He asks penetrating questions that quickly get to the heart of the matter and probe deeply into circumstances and motives:

- In the Garden, God asked Adam and Eve, "Where are you?" (Genesis 3:9 ESV)

- Cain was asked, "Where is Abel your brother?" (Genesis 4:8 ESV)

- God asked Abraham, "Why did Sarah laugh and say, 'Shall I indeed bear a child, now that I am old?'" (Genesis 18:13 ESV)

- Job was asked, "Where were you when I laid the foundation of the earth?" (Job 38:4 ESV)

- When in a storm on a boat, Jesus asked the disciples, "Why are you afraid?" (Matthew 8:26 ESV)

- When people were discussing whether Jesus was John the Baptist, Elijah, Jeremiah, or one of the prophets, Jesus asked his disciples, "But who do you say that I am?" (Matthew 16:15 ESV)

- When the disciples had been arguing over who would be the greatest in God's kingdom, Jesus asked, "What were you discussing on the way?" (Mark 9:33 ESV)

- The scribes and the Pharisees were asked by Jesus, "Why do you question in your hearts? Which is easier, to say, 'Your sins are forgiven you,' or to say, 'Rise and walk'?" (Luke 5:22–23 ESV)

- Jesus asked Andrew and John, "What are you seeking?" (John 1:38 ESV)

Knowledge and Skills

The identification of the necessary knowledge and skills that need to be taught is the last component of an Understanding by Design unit of instruction. At this point, teachers should be asking themselves the question, "What knowledge and skills will students need to be able to understand the big idea and related enduring understandings?" Students still need to acquire foundational knowledge and skills over the course of their time in school. Wiggins and McTighe's position is that these need to be taught, but only when they are nested under the umbrella of big ideas.

Understanding

Understanding is a complex issue. Because there are various aspects of understanding, there have been several attempts at defining understanding. For example, in 1956, Benjamin Bloom created definitions to categorize degrees of cognitive complexity of assessment items on university exams. His six categories are well known as Bloom's taxonomy: knowledge, comprehension, application, analysis, synthesis, and evaluation. Over the course of time, a ladder view of cognition evolved, and Bloom's taxonomy has been used to support this concept of learning, even though that was never Bloom's intent for one element to be considered more important than another.

"My son, if you receive my words, and treasure my commands within you, so that you incline your ear to wisdom, and apply your heart to understanding . . . then you will understand the fear of Lord."
—PROVERBS 2:1–2, 5

Wiggins and McTighe's definition of understanding is to make sense of what one knows, to be able to know why it is so, and to have the ability to use it in various situations and contexts. They believed that understanding involves sophisticated insights and abilities reflected in varied performances and contexts, that different kinds of understanding exist, and that knowledge and skill do not automatically lead to understanding. The more we see a student able to explain, apply, and offer multiple points of view on the same idea, the more likely it is that the student understands that idea.

Some ways that understanding is shown are outlined in the next table.

Indicators of Deep Understanding	Indicators of a Little Knowledge but not Deep Understanding
Student can	Student can
• Explain things clearly and completely • Teach others effectively • Apply their understanding flexibly in new situations (transfer) • Analyze and evaluate information and sources • Justify and support their ideas • Interpret meaning of things such as text, data, and experiences • Generate new questions • Recognize different points of view on an issue • Diagnose errors and correct them • Self-assess and monitor their progress • Reflect on their learning	• Give back what they were told • Plug in • Remember • Select the "correct" answer from given alternatives • Apply a skill only in the way that it was learned

Jay McTighe and Judy Willis, *Upgrade Your Teaching: Understanding by Design Meets Neuroscience, ASCD, 2019, pp. 27–28.*

In order to better clarify the meaning of understanding, they identified six facets of understanding: explanation, application, interpretation, perspective, empathy, and self-knowledge. The chart shows Wiggins and McTighe's definitions of each of these six facets:

UbD Six Facets of Understanding

Explanation	Providing thorough, supported, and justifiable accounts of phenomena, facts, and data
Interpretation	Finding meaning, significance, sense, or value in human experience, ideas, events, data, and texts. It is to tell a good story, provide powerful metaphors, images, anecdotes, analogies, and/or models.
Application	Effectively using and adapting what we know in diverse contexts
Perspective	Seeing points of view, with critical eyes and ears; seeing the big picture
Empathy	Getting inside, finding value in what others might find odd, alien, or implausible; perceiving sensitively, based on prior direct experience
Self-Knowledge	Perceiving the personal style, prejudices, projections, and habits of mind that both shape and impede our own understanding; being aware of what we do not understand, and why it is so hard to understand.

Adapted from Wiggins and McTighe, *Understanding by Design*, p. 84

Explanation, application, and interpretation have much in common with Bloom's taxonomy. However, perspective, empathy, and self-knowledge are also characteristics that are important and greatly valued in today's world.

From a Christian standpoint, the six facets of understanding are a much better match for analysis of understanding than Bloom's taxonomy. God is deeply interested in the development of each individual's character. The ultimate change in perspective comes when we decide to rely on God rather than rely on ourselves for wisdom and guidance.

For a school to intentionally aid students in developing their abilities to deal with different perspectives, have empathy for others, and better understand who they are in Christ would be a welcome change from the knowledge- and skills-based curriculum that pervades many schools, including Christian schools. A goal in UbD-planned units is that, over the course of a year, students will be challenged to grow in each of the six facets. Often, the attributes related to a school's mission statement can be easily aligned to one of these six facets.

The traditional knowledge and skills that are taught in schools today still hold significant importance. Knowledge, or what we want students to know, includes vocabulary, terminology, definitions, key facts, formulas, critical details, important events and people, and sequences and timelines.

Skills, or what we want students to be able to do, includes such necessary abilities as computation skills, decoding, listening, speaking, writing, thinking, research, study skills, and interpersonal skills.

Teachers need to decide in each unit which sets of knowledge and skills need to be taught, but they need to be nested under the umbrella of the big ideas, enduring understanding, essential question(s), and the facets of understanding.

An Example of Stage 1

Teachers often comment after writing Stage 1 (identify the desired learning results) using the Understanding by Design framework that it takes more time than they expected, but they have better clarity about what is most important in the unit. There is no right or wrong way to structure the document, but Wiggins and McTighe have offered several different templates over the years to aid teachers in the development process. If writing UbD units is schoolwide practice, using similar templates is helpful for a peer review process.

Following is an example of a Stage 1 document from a Christian school fifth grade class. Both character development and leadership were called out by the school's mission statement and portrait of graduate statements. The big idea of the unit was courage.

Stage 1—Identify Desired Results

Big Idea: Courage

Graduate Attributes:

● Growing Spiritually

● Productive Thinkers

○ Effective Action

○ Effective Relationships

○ Lifelong Learner

Standard(s):

Reading

Writing

Listening and Speaking

Language

Understanding(s):

Students will understand that . . .

Overarching enduring understanding(s):

Being a leader often requires a person to act courageously.

Personal loss is one of God's ways to help us to learn to rely on him, which is an important source of courage.

Topical enduring understanding(s):

Courage is being able to look beyond our circumstances and trust that God has all things under control.

Courage is often developed by trusting that God is in control and will never forsake you in any situation (2 Corinthians 1:9).

Essential Question(s):

Overarching essential question(s):

Does leadership require courage?

Why does God allow people to go through difficult situations?

Topical essential questions(s):

What does courage look like?

Can courage be developed and strengthened in a person? How or why?

(Knowledge) Student will know . . .

the location of Sudan and Kenya in Africa.

the key elements of an obituary.

(Skills) Students will be able to . . .

Reading Literature

Quote accurately from a text when explaining what the text says explicitly and when drawing inferences from the text.

Reading Informational Text

Determine two or more main ideas of a text and explain how they are supported by key details; summarize the text.

Determine the plot, character, setting, and theme of a story.

Write a character analysis of a character in a story.

Explain the cause and effect in a story.

Make predictions about a story.

Writing

Write opinion pieces on topics or texts, supporting a point of view with reasons and information.

- Introduce a topic or text clearly, state an opinion, and create an organizational structure in which ideas are logically grouped to support the writer's purpose. Provide logically ordered reasons that are supported by facts and details.
- Link opinion and reasons using words, phrases, and clauses (e.g., consequently, specifically).
- Provide a concluding statement or section related to the opinion presented.

Speaking and Listening

Comprehension and Collaboration: Engage effectively in a range of collaborative discussions (one-on-one, in groups, and teacher-led) with diverse partners on grade 5 topics and texts, building on others' ideas and expressing their own clearly.

- Come to discussions prepared, having read or studied required material; explicitly draw on that preparation and other information known about the topic to explore ideas under discussion.
- Follow agreed-upon rules for discussions and carry out assigned roles.
- Pose and respond to specific questions by making comments that contribute to the discussion and elaborate on the remarks of others.
- Review the key ideas expressed and draw conclusions in light of information and knowledge gained from the discussions.

Language

Conventions of Standard English

- Demonstrate command of the conventions of standard English capitalization, punctuation, and spelling when writing.
- Use punctuation to separate items in a series.
- Use a comma to separate an introductory element from the rest of the sentence.
- Use commas to set off the words "yes" and "no" (e.g., Yes, thank you), to set off a tag question from the rest of the sentence (e.g., It's true, isn't it?), and to indicate direct address (e.g., Is that you, Steve?).
- Use underlining, quotation marks, or italics to indicate titles of works.
- Spell grade-appropriate words correctly, consulting references as needed.

Key Chapter Takeaways

✓ Teaching for understanding and transfer requires a shift in teacher's instructional planning.

✓ Stage 1 of Understanding by Design is an opportunity for teachers to intentionally link instruction with the school's mission.

✓ Enduring understandings and the related essential questions are ideal opportunities for teachers to integrate Bible teachings into units of instruction.

✓ Clearly identifying the big idea and enduring understandings of a unit helps teachers clarify what is most important and aids students in organizing knowledge and skills in ways that the brain prefers for better long-term memory.

✓ Essential questions are tools to engage students and when revisited over a course of a unit cultivate reflection, rethinking, and revision by students.

✓ The six facets of understanding include three aspects of understanding (perspective, empathy, and self-knowledge) that match biblical values.

✓ Knowledge and skills are still important elements in an Understanding by Design unit, but only when under the umbrella of big ideas and enduring understandings.

Concluding Thoughts

This level of thoughtful planning (employing the use of big ideas, enduring understandings, essential questions, the six facets of understanding, knowledge, and skills) results in better alignment within units of instruction. Also, teachers at the Christian school can regularly embed the mission-related outcomes into the enduring understandings of their units of instruction.

"My son, if you receive my words, and treasure my commands within you, so that you incline your ear to wisdom, and apply your heart to understanding . . . then you will understand the fear of Lord."

—PROVERBS 2:1–2, 5

"Happy is the man who finds wisdom, and the man who gains understanding."

—PROVERBS 3:13

Understanding is much deeper than knowledge. There are many who know but few who understand!

Educator Interview

Q: As a secondary-level Christian school teacher, how has Understanding by Design (UbD) impacted your planning for instruction?

A: It has made me much more intentional in my learning activities. Before UbD, I used to look at the material I needed to cover and then divide it into teachable sections; there was not a lot of intentionality behind anything. Now, in light of UbD and backward design, I list the outcomes (big ideas, transfer goals, and understandings) I want the students to take away from my class. I then incorporate materials and learning activities to support these outcomes. It is quite a liberating process. I no longer worry about how much I need to cover. Instead, I look for signs that the students understand the desired outcomes and use this to inform what else needs to be covered.

Q: What was the greatest challenge for you when you first tried using the UbD framework to plan units of instruction using big ideas, enduring understandings, essential questions, performance tasks, and rubrics?

A: This was totally new for me, and the greatest challenge I faced was planning backward. When I started with the end in mind, I was overwhelmed by the enormous task I had set out to accomplish. It was the first time I was trying to plan out my instruction weeks in advance. It required a pretty steep learning curve. At first, it was a fairly arduous task, but the more I used the framework and became more comfortable with it, the planning became quite enjoyable. Now, I could not imagine doing things a different way. I find it fun to plan

Secondary Teacher

HEATH ANNETT

Bio

English & Bible Teacher
Teacher Leader
BA, Biblical Literature,
    Northwest University
MA, Biblical Exegesis,
    Wheaton College

units now, so much so that I sometimes do it as an activity to pass the time; it does not feel like work!

Q: How did your students first react to your new instructional approach? What happened as they became more comfortable focusing on understanding rather than just knowledge and skill attainment?

A: At first, they struggled quite a bit. When I used my first-ever UbD unit in English 7, my students asked me if we were going to do any *real* work and requested worksheets! After their initial shock, they seemed to adjust quite quickly to the new approach. I have found that by giving students more time to reflect and work on authentic performance tasks instead of knowledge- and skill-based assignments, they think more about what they are doing. I have seen the students reflect and interact more with the material and fellow classmates across the board.

Q: As a teacher leader at your school, with what issues do you see teachers needing the most support when trying to write and implement UbD-based units?

A: When switching to UbD-based units, teachers need encouragement. It can be quite a difficult and stressful endeavor. Teachers need to know that the process takes time and that units do not need to be perfect the first time. Teachers should not view it as additional work to what they currently do, but that will eventually supersede their current learning plan. It is crucial to take plenty of time to develop units at the onset to start the process.

We have also found that teachers respond well to praise and recognition from peers and administration when they produce high-quality units. Administration's support is also a great motivation and must not be understated. At our school, administration decided to reward teachers with cash bonuses as incentive for writing and completing units. Many teachers have taken advantage of this and are producing high-quality units.

Q: What advice would you have for teachers first starting out when planning units using the UbD framework?

A: When teachers begin this process, they must work hard at not falling back into old routines. My advice would be to just dive on in and trust the process. At first a teacher may have a hard time, thinking that moving away from skills- and knowledge-based instruction will have a negative impact on student learning. In actuality, the exact opposite is true. When students finally grasp the concept of understanding-based learning, it is like turning on a lightbulb. Once they get it, they get it, and the learning process will start to take on an entirely different shape that is both enriching and authentic. While challenging at first, UbD framework provides a plethora of rich opportunities for learning.

4

Assessing for What Is Most Important

*The power of assessment is in the ongoing assessment
not the summative assessment.*

—JAY MCTIGHE

AN UNUSUAL ASPECT OF Understanding by Design is its backward design process. In Stage 2–Determine Acceptable Evidence, teachers develop assessments prior to writing a learning plan. This seems like the reverse order to most educators. Teachers are asked to carefully determine a range of assessments, not just the summative test at the end of the unit. This broader view of assessment results in a wide range of formats included in each unit. No one assessment can give a complete picture of a student's development; different tests provide different information.

In Stage 2 of UbD, teachers are encouraged to select assessments that best match the particular purpose. For example, the standard true-false/multiple-choice/matching test or quiz is an efficient and effective tool for determining student progress on knowledge and skills. Using rich performance tasks works best to gain insight into students' understanding of a concept. Or when teachers want students to work on their higher-order thinking skill of self-assessment, they use some form of a reflection with students. The graphic shows where these types of assessment fit the best.

Moving Learning Forward in Christian Schools

STAGE TWO
ASSESSMENT METHODS

**EACH ASSESSMENT METHOD HAS AN APPROPRIATE TIME AND
PLACE IN STAGE 2 – COLLECTION OF EVIDENCE**

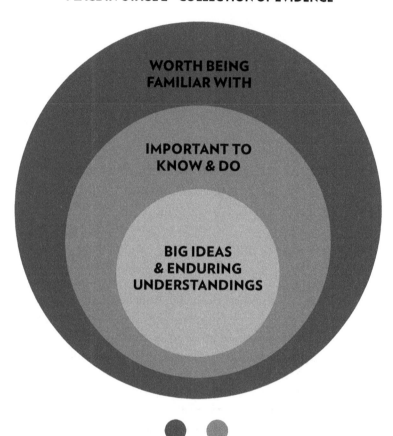

WORTH BEING
FAMILIAR WITH

IMPORTANT TO
KNOW & DO

BIG IDEAS
& ENDURING
UNDERSTANDINGS

TRADITIONAL QUIZZES & TESTS
Paper and pencil, selected response, constructed response

PERFORMANCE TASKS & PROJECTS
Complex, open-ended, authentic

Based on data from Jay McTighe & Grant Wiggins, *Understanding by Design 2nd Edition*, ASCD, 2005,
p. 170.

In the end, the hope in developing UbD assessments that provide valid and reliable evidence is that students understand the big idea and related enduring understandings, along with the fact that they have attained the necessary knowledge and skills (the desired learning results). Typically, in classrooms today, assessments most often employed are standard tests and quizzes to measure student success or failure to attain knowledge and skills. Consequently, the message given to students is that knowledge and skills are all that is important. This runs counter to what schools have usually stated in their mission statements where the most important student outcomes are being effective communicators, contributing citizens, spiritually mature, good collaborators, critical thinkers, etc.

An additional benefit of developing assessments earlier in the unit-planning process is that when teachers work on their lesson plans in Stage 3, their instruction ends up being more focused on the things they know they are going to assess.

Assessing for Understanding and Transfer

Including assessments for understanding and transfer of mission-related outcomes sends the message that these things are equally important. Teachers are then able to ascertain and have evidence of student understanding and transfer. When the key outcomes from the mission are consistently addressed in units of instruction and related performance tasks are used to gather evidence, then a school has established a strong link between what it says are the most important goals of the organization and what regularly occurs in the instructional program.

> The illiterate of the future will not be the person that cannot read.
> It will be the person who does not learn.
>
> —ALAN TOFFLER

Assessing for understanding and/or transfer requires teachers to not only rethink what is important to assessment, but also to develop a broader set of skills with regard to developing assessments. McTighe uses the phrase "knowing is binary but understanding is by degree." By definition, binary is a numeric system that only uses two digits, 0 and 1. Computers operate in a binary manner, meaning they store data and perform calculations using only zeros and ones. In the assessment arena, this means something is either right or wrong. This arena is where traditional classroom assessments work best. But when it comes to determining at what level a student understands something, assessment is more complicated and requires different tools of evaluation. Performance tasks are excellent tools to reveal the degree of student understanding.

Developing Performance Tasks

Understanding can be determined if students can exhibit the ability to transfer big ideas, knowledge, and skills on challenging performance tasks. Wiggins and McTighe define performance tasks as complex challenges that mirror the issues and problems faced by adults. Brain research has discovered that the more authentic a task feels, the more the brain engages, which increases the chances for better long-term memory.

Therefore, trying to make performance mirror real-life circumstances is a productive strategy in learning. There is no formulaic and set model for performance tasks. They can range in length from short-term tasks to long-term, multistaged projects. The end result can be one or multiple products and/or performances.

To aid teachers in the creation of performance tasks, Wiggins and McTighe designed the acronym GRASPS in an effort to remind teachers of elements that help establish some form of authenticity.

G—Goal

R—Role

A—Audience

S—Situation

P—Product/Performance and Purpose

S—Standards and Criteria for Success

Standards and Criteria for Success

When developing performance tasks, it is useful to consider how the UbD six facets of understanding could be applied. For example, if one of the unit's enduring understandings is that students are asked to see a historical event from a different perspective than is typically presented in a textbook, then a performance task could be designed for students to write or present a speech on this same topic from another point of view (e.g., the loser in a war or major political dilemma). Again, the goal of Stage 2 planning is to derive evidence of the desired learning results from Stage 1. If one of the major goals of Stage 1 is to work on the higher-order thinking skill of seeing issues from various perspectives, then a performance task that reveals how much is understood about perspective and how students can transfer that into a new situation is fitting. The *Understanding by Design: Professional Development Workbook* provides useful starter verbs and examples.[1]

An Example of Stage 2

Again, like Stage 1 using the Understanding by Design framework, developing Stage 2 takes a little more time than previously experienced by teachers. But the end result is improved unity between Stage 1—Identify Desired Learning Results and Stage 2–Determine Acceptable Evidence.

Let's examine an example of Stage 2 from the same fifth grade unit on courage shown in Chapter 3. The Stage 2 performance task centered on the main character (Salva) from the book *A Long Walk to Water*. The main character exhibited unusual courage during the time of civil war in Sudan.

First using the GRASPS acronym, the teacher outlined the performance task:

- Goal: Write an obituary

- Role: Writer

- Audience: Family, friends, and community members

- Situation: Salva died and his family is looking for someone to write his obituary

- Product/Performance and Purpose: Newspaper obituary

- Standards and Criteria for Success:

---

1. A full treatment of how to develop performance tasks is not in the scope of this book. Jay McTighe and Grant Wiggins' book *Understanding by Design: Professional Development Workbook*, ASCD, 2004, provides many pages of tools for teachers. There are lists of student roles and audiences, possible products and performances, and starter phrases for constructing each element of GRASPS, along with sample performance tasks by discipline.

- Understanding the development of courage and leadership
- Understanding that God is the source of courage
- Writing and language
- Elements of an obituary

Below is an example of a Stage 2 planning template for this unit.

Stage 2—Determine Acceptable Evidence

Performance Task(s):

Your job is to write an obituary for Salva. He has reached the end of his life, and you are charged with summarizing his life experiences for an obituary for your local newspaper. Keep in mind that the readers who will be most interested in your writing will be family members and friends. Also, community members will be interested in reading about Salva because of the many things he accomplished and experiences he faced throughout his life.

Rubric:

○ Analytic

● Holistic

Facets of Understanding

● Explanation

○ Interpretation

○ Application

● Perspective

○ Empathy

● Self-Knowledge

Other Evidence:

Worksheet—Identify Plot, Characters, Setting, and Theme

Exercise—Retell in Pictures

Exercise—Timeline for *A Long Walk to Water*

Venn Diagram—Character Comparison for *A Long Walk to Water* and *David and Goliath*

Vocabulary Collection for *A Long Walk to Water*

Worksheet—Making Inferences

Worksheet—Cause and Effect

Worksheet—Prediction/Anticipation Guide

Weekly Reflections

Academic Prompts—Response to Literature

Reflection Methods

● Journal/Learning Log

○ Focus Group Discussion

● Whole Class Discussion

○ Fish Bowl Discussion

○ Other

Evaluating Performance Tasks with Rubrics

If we accept that knowing is binary but understanding is by degree, traditional assessments yield little information regarding understanding. Rubrics are an excellent option for teachers to use to ascertain the level of student understanding. Well-developed rubrics provide both valid and reliable evidence of student performance. Neurologically, rubrics provide a template onto which students can link new learning when their brains recognize the categories of stored knowledge they relate to.[2]

A rubric should be developed in conjunction with the performance task with clear and appropriate criteria. Rubrics are not a set of directions set into a chart or counting up parts or components. The criteria should reveal the degree of understanding. There should be descriptions of levels of performance quality for each criterion to determine levels of understanding.

The criteria should focus on the understanding rather than on the task. In *How to Create and Use Rubrics: For Formative Assessment and Grading*, 2013, Susan Brookhart describes the characteristics of high-quality rubrics:

- Appropriate: Each criterion represents an enduring understanding or aspect of the grade-level expectations.

- Definable: Each criterion has a clear meaning that both students and teachers understand.

- Observable: Each criterion describes a quality in the performance that can be seen or heard by others.

- Distinct from one another: Each criterion identifies a separate aspect of the product or performance.

- Complete: All criteria together describe the whole of the learning.

- Able to support a description along a continuum of quality: Each criterion can be described over a range of performance levels.[3]

Two ways to describe rubrics are holistic and analytic. Holistic rubrics provide an overall impression of a student's work in a single score best used at the end of a performance task. Analytic rubrics offer detailed feedback on important various aspects of the performance task.

Analytic feedback can be used when students use the rubric for self-assessment or peer review of another student's work. Or a teacher could

2. Goodrich, "Understanding Rubrics," 15.

3. Brookhart, *Create & Use Rubrics*, 25.

use the rubric to give students analytic feedback and allow opportunity for revision.

Holistic feedback is best suited for the final product or performance. This can be conducted by both the student and/or the teacher.

Jay McTighe and Judy Willis have identified several benefits of using rubrics. Rubrics

- provide specific feedback on specific salient traits of performance;

- serve as evaluative tools to measure and grade student learning;

- can be used as learning targets for students, which helps learners to recognize the qualities needed;

- foster the development of a "growth mindset" by revealing the relationship between effort and progress; and

- can be used for student self- or peer assessment, thereby developing executive functions of goal directing, critical analyzing, and self-monitoring.[4]

Levels of performance should be descriptions of performance, not evaluative (excellent, good, average, poor). In descriptions of performance, the levels should clearly delineate different possible outcomes.

Review the rubric for the fifth grade performance task from the unit on courage mentioned previously. A teacher could use this rubric for either analytic or holistic evaluation.

	Exceeds Grade Level Expectations	Meets Grade Level Expectations	Approaching Grade Level Expectations	Below Grade Level Expectations
Understanding of the development of courage and leadership	I know a lot about, and in my writing show, how courage and leadership are developed.	My paper shows a general understanding of how courage and leadership are developed.	I attempt to explain my limited understanding of how courage and leadership are developed, but my details are unclear or confusing.	My paper shares little or no information about how courage and leadership are developed.

4. McTighe and Willis, *UbD Meets Neuroscience*, 88.

	Exceeds Grade Level Expectations	Meets Grade Level Expectations	Approaching Grade Level Expectations	Below Grade Level Expectations
Understanding that God is the source of real courage	I was able to cite clear evidence from Salva's life that God was the source of his courage.	I was able to cite suitable evidence from Salva's life that God was the source of his courage.	I was able to cite some evidence from Salva's life that God was the source of his courage.	I was able to cite little or no evidence from Salva's life that God was the source of his courage.
Writing	My ideas are very clear and supported with accurate textual evidence such as details, information, and inferences from the story.	My ideas are clear and supported with appropriate textual evidence such as details, information, and inferences from the story.	My ideas are supported with minimal textual evidence such as details, information, and inferences from the story.	My ideas are supported with little or no textual evidence such as details, information, and inferences from the story.
Elements of an Obituary	Obituary includes all key elements as well as appropriately honors Salva's life: Announcement of death Key dates: birth, death Family Life achievements Disappointments Funeral arrangements	Obituary includes satisfactory number of key elements as well as appropriately honors Salva's life: Announcement of death Key dates: birth, death Family Life achievements Disappointments Funeral arrangements	Obituary includes limited key elements of Salva's life: Announcement of death Key dates: birth, death Family Life achievements Disappointments Funeral arrangements	Obituary includes few or no key elements of Salva's life: Announcement of death Key dates: birth, death Family Life achievements Disappointments Funeral arrangements

	Exceeds Grade Level Expectations	Meets Grade Level Expectations	Approaching Grade Level Expectations	Below Grade Level Expectations
Mechanics	My spelling is accurate. I paid close attention to punctuation. I used capitals correctly. The minimal or no errors do not interfere with understanding of the writing. More than three paragraphs are present, and each one is indented to show where a new idea begins.	My spelling is mostly accurate. I paid attention to punctuation. Most sentences and proper nouns begin with capitals. The few errors do not interfere with understanding of the writing. At least three paragraphs are present and indented.	Spelling errors are common. Punctuation is basic, but I need to use commas to improve my writing. Most sentences but few proper nouns begin with capitals. Errors interfere with understanding of the writing. At least one paragraph is present. Others might not all begin in the right spots.	Spelling errors are frequent, even on simple words. Punctuation is limited and makes reading this paper difficult. Capital letters are scattered all over or not at all. I haven't spent much time editing this paper. I haven't gotten the hang of paragraphs yet.

Here are some tips for designing and using rubrics:

- Include the significant traits of the enduring understanding(s) in the rubric, not just traits that are easiest to score.

- Use kid-friendly language, especially for younger students.

- Present the rubric early in the unit to the students, so the expectations are clear.

- Provide the rubric in advance of the assessment along with exemplars and/or anchors.

- Help students see the rubric as a guide to success.[5]

5. McTighe and Willis, *UbD Meets Neuroscience*, 88–89.

Anchors and Exemplars

Providing students with examples of previous student work is another way to cultivate understanding. Just like rubrics, the anchors and exemplars aid students in seeing what is expected in the performance task. When teachers walk pupils through another student's work using the rubric as a road map and pointing out the aspects that meet each area, students are being taught how to see details that make a difference.

Expert learners have the ability to discriminate details and address specific expectations. Because the teachers are expert learners, they can provide written annotations about each anchor and/or exemplar for students. In the end, the goal is for all students to learn the secrets of how the brain works best and to be able to build the necessary pathways within the brain for long-term memory.

The next pages show an example of an anchor paper from the fifth-grade class from the performance task on courage.

The student scored a "Meets Grade-Level Expectations" on this performance task. These are some of the annotations:

> The student's ideas were clear and were supported with appropriate textual details and information from the story. Spelling and punctuation were mostly accurate. There were at least three paragraphs, and the sentences and proper nouns began with capitals. The key elements of an obituary were present: announcement of death, dates of birth and death, family names, life achievements, disappointments, and funeral arrangements. A general understanding of how courage and leadership are developed was implied, but there were no references to God having a part in developing courage.

This example shows how a Christian school collected evidence of students' understanding about the importance of developing godly leadership (which was one of the school's mission-related outcomes).

Salva Marien Dut Ariik

Salva Marien Dut Ariik was born in Lou Ariik in 1979. He died in a car crash on November 5, 2013 in Rochester New York. He had many challenges in his life, like almost being killed a lot of times. Some of the schools Salva went to are Lou Ariik Elementry, and a university and some schools in refugee camps.

Salva had three Sudanese brothers Kuoi, Ring and Ariik. Salva has two sets of parents his foster parents are Chris and Louise his Sudanese father is Mawien Dut Ariik. Salva made many friends throughout his journey two of his friends were Marial who was killed by a lion and Busha who helped Salva find a bee hive.

Some of Salvas life achievements are running out into the bush and later finding his uncle, who became the troop leader in Salvas group. Salvas uncle encouraged Salva by keeping him alive. There would be a rock or a tree and Salvas uncle would say you just need to go as far as that rock. Then after Salva reached to that rock then Salvas uncle would say the same thing. Salva used that technique when he was guiding his group. So Salvas uncle helped Salva become a leader.

Some of Salvas dissapointments are he lost friends and family. He also died at the age of thirty four. Here are three great words to sum up Salvas life unbelievable,

amazing and brave, Salvas memorial service
will be held at Rochester Funeral Home
on November 20, 2013 at 11:30.

Student Reporting Systems

Because there is much emphasis on grades, report cards, and transcripts in today's educational world, teachers understandably want to immediately link the evaluative tools to a grade. The goal of Stage 2 is collecting evidence of learning, so grading is not the primary task at this point.

As the unit unfolds, using the assessments to provide feedback to students is a vital component of the learning process. It is unfortunate that the grades from today's student reporting systems are what students most care about, not the learning. Many students do not consider work important unless it is going to be graded.

The reporting system has so warped their view of what school is about that they have lost sight of the fact that being interested in learning and being a lifelong learner may be two of the most important outcomes that could be attained in life. Once instruction has begun on the unit, then it is time for teachers to consider incorporating the evidence into a grade or mark.

In Chapter 6, there will be a more in-depth systemic look at a student reporting system (report cards, conferences, progress reports, and portfolios) that aligns with an instructional program and includes a focus on the school's mission and the resulting information regarding students' understanding and transfer.

Key Chapter Takeaways

✓ Using a wide range of assessment tools over the course of a unit provides teachers multiple insights into how students are learning and understanding.

✓ Performance tasks are tools to reveal the degree of student understanding and transfer.

✓ Authenticity in performance tasks increases the chances of long-term memory.

✓ Rubrics are excellent tools for determining the standards and criteria for success.

✓ Anchors and exemplars provide students with a road map by pointing out the elements that are important for each area.

Concluding Thoughts

Being thoughtful and careful when collecting evidence is the hallmark of high-quality Understanding by Design units. Implementing assessments that focus on the learning rather than grades speaks an important message to students. Collecting evidence that reveals how students are doing with achieving the school's mission should be a top priority in every Christian school.

A teacher affects eternity. He can never tell where his influence stops.

—HENRY B. ADAMS

Educator Interview

Q: As a teacher in a Christian elementary school, how has Understanding by Design (UbD) impacted your planning for instruction?

A: It has allowed me to focus on what is important and what is not. Before learning to create UbD units, I would often just teach the book. I can now concentrate on what is important for building understanding.

Q: What was the greatest challenge for you when you first tried using the UbD framework to plan units of instruction using big ideas, enduring understandings, essential questions, performance tasks, and rubrics?

A: This was totally new for me, and starting with the end was confusing at first. As I had mostly taught from the written curriculum, I never thought about what the end should look like. I had written rubrics and had assigned projects before, but I am not sure I can say they actually assessed what I was trying to teach my students.

Elementary Teacher

OLIVER BLACK

Bio

Fifth Grade Christian School
  Teacher
Teacher Leader
BA, Bible and Theology, William
  Jessup University
MEd, Teaching and Learning,
  Liberty University

Q: How did your students first react to your new instructional approach? What happened as they became more comfortable focusing on understanding rather than just knowledge and skill attainment?

A: The students kept asking if what we were learning was going to be on the test. I'd also say that, since they were used to "dessert" projects, they didn't take their work as seriously as they could have. But as they became more used to the methods of UbD, they became more engaged. Focusing on understanding also has the interesting byproduct of increasing retention of knowledge and skills. Since they had a framework for understanding the material, their retention was far better.

Q: **As a teacher-leader at your Christian school, what issues do you see teachers needing the most support with when trying to write and implement UbD-based units?**

A: It is not the same for all teachers. For me, Stage 1 was the hardest, because I'd never really thought about the end product. Other teachers at our school had no problem with Stage 1. I noticed Stage 2 being difficult for some, because it can be difficult to align a project/performance task with goals. It was important for them to know that not every performance task had to be a two-week-long project, and you don't have to assess all of the understanding in just one performance task. Stage 3 can also be a challenge, because without explicit instruction, teachers will just keep doing what they have done before.

Q: **What advice would you have for teachers first starting out when planning units using the UbD framework?**

A: Don't give up! Take it slow. It will seem impossible at first, but after some practice, it's as easy as writing any other unit, but with more fruit for your labor. On the more practical side, looking at a list of possible roles for the students and audience is a great place to get inspiration for designing a performance task.

5

Lessons for the Twenty-First Century

Many things can wait; the child cannot. Now is the time his
bones are formed; his mind is being developed. To him,
we cannot say tomorrow; his name is today.

—GABRIELA MISTRAL, CHILEAN POET
AND NOBEL LAUREATE

CREATING THE DAY-TO-DAY LESSONS for a unit of instruction is what
teachers often most enjoy and are experts at. In fact, when teachers are not
good at this aspect of their jobs, their classrooms are usually either chaotic
or needing more instructional focus. Fortunately, this is the exception in
education.

Excellent teachers regularly work on improving their lesson design
and instructional strategies, as they see professional growth as part of being
a learner. So, when planning the daily lessons, what areas of instruction
should teachers be thinking about to improve student learning? Knowing
that what is expected of today's graduates is different than it was in the past,
how should teacher lessons be altered? Knowing that in the US classroom,
there is often a great diversity of students, what needs to be adjusted in instruction? Or with students often being more technology-savvy than their
teachers, how do teachers keep students engaged?

When schools flourish, all flourishes.

—MARTIN LUTHER

For example, if we know that the brain has preferences and priorities, then it is incumbent on teachers to take advantage of this knowledge about the brain. As noted in Chapter 2, engaging in the process of learning actually increases one's capacity to learn. There are several strategies that increase transfer of learning from working memory to long-term memory that teachers can intentionally employ into their lessons:

- using multiple senses
- novel and/or unexpected events
- thought-provoking questions
- experiential learning
- emotionally significant events
- relating learning to previous learning
- relationships and/or patterns

If physical activity aids in learning, then should we not consider how to implement this into our school and classrooms? If the brain needs periodic rests during the day to be able to receive information, then should teachers not consider ways to embed this relief into the instructional process for students to recharge?

In Stage 3 of Understanding by Design, Planning Learning Experiences and Instruction, teachers are provided a host of reminders of quality instructional strategies that are consistent with current brain research and best practices. In Stage 1 and Stage 2, the planning revolves around content and assessments. Stage 3 is the time for teachers to think carefully about their students. Each group of students has its own sets of strengths and weaknesses and personality. This can be so impactful that secondary-level teachers need to know that they must use different strategies when teaching the same unit to a group of students in the morning versus in the late afternoon. In addition, students with special needs may also require a change in approach.

WHERETO

The goal of the learning plan is to aid students in achieving the desired learning results outlined in Stage 1 of UbD. Wiggins and McTighe created the acronym WHERETO to prompt teachers during their development of their learning plan in Stage 3.

W–Where, Why, What

H–Hook and Hold

E–Equip, Explore, and Experience

R–Reflect, Rethink, and Revise

E–Evaluate

T–Tailor

O–Organize

These aspects of the learning plan do not appear in every lesson during the unit and are not laid out in a sequential manner but provide teachers with reminders about building long-term memory practices into the unit. For example, if we know that the brain is goal-oriented, then giving students insight into where the unit is going, why it is important, and what is most important effectively uses their brains' natural inclinations. In 2019, McTighe and Willis offered other practical suggestions.[1]

- Directly state learning goals at the beginning of the unit.
- Show how student work is related to the goals.
- Explain the rationale and relevance of the unit goals.
- Invite students to generate questions about the unit (KWL).
- Ask students to identify personal learning goals.
- Post and discuss essential questions.
- Present culminating performance task requirements.
- Review carefully scoring rubrics.
- Show models or exemplars of the performance task.

1. McTighe and Willis, *Upgrade Your Teaching,* 53–56. It is not in the scope of this book to cover all the definitions and insights into each element of WHERETO, but this can be found in McTighe and Wiggins, *Understanding by Design,* 2005, and McTighe and Willis, *Upgrade Your Teaching: Understanding by Design Meets Neuroscience,* 2019.

Wiggins and McTighe also challenge teachers to look at planning their learning through the lens of roles that teachers can take on over the course of a unit:

- direct instructor and model
- facilitator
- coach

Their view is that these are not an either/or option, but each provides opportunity to increase the chances of achieving long-term memory. When teachers are in the direct instruction and modeling mode, they are attempting to help students acquire knowledge and skills. The facilitator approach is best for provoking students to make meaning of what they are learning. When teachers act as coaches, students are best able to transfer knowledge and skills.

The goal in this lens for planning learning is for teachers to design for each type of role and related learning. The McTighe and Willis book *Upgrade Your Teaching: Understanding by Design Meets Neuroscience* has a thorough treatment of each of these elements.

Teachers often comment after writing Stage 3 that they were more focused on specific outcomes than they were previously when using the Understanding by Design framework. Again, there is no right or wrong way to structure Stage 3. Some teachers like a day-by-day format while others use a more narrative approach. Having the Stage 3 section be a useful and practical document for teachers is what is most important. Keeping notes of what worked well and what needs to be revised is vital. Ideas for improvement can be quickly lost in a teacher's busy, jam-packed, fast-paced schedule. It also usually takes several renditions of a UbD unit before teachers find that they are pleased with it and find the unit yields maximum student learning.

Once Stage 3 is written, a productive strategy for teachers to conduct is to review the unit and identify at what juncture each of the WHERETO elements occurred and/or when the students were given the opportunity to acquire knowledge and skills, make meaning of the content, and transfer their learning.

An Example of Stage 3

This is an example of Stage 3 from the same fifth grade unit on courage shown in Chapters 3 and 4.

Stage 3—Establish Learning Plan

Learning Activities:

Day 1:

Anticipatory guide: before and after 'Water Walk'

Journal prompt: Write a paragraph describing your thoughts and feelings regarding water activities of today.

Create posters predicting challenges/obstacles for Nya and Salva; present posters to class.

Day 2:

Show "Salva's Story"

(https://www.youtube.com/watch?v=cuLbHz7k9xg)

Intro essential questions

Intro and share background—*A Long Walk to Water* by Linda Sue Park

Read Chapter 1—whole group

Cover tenses/points of view

Assign at-home reading—Chapter 2

Day 3:

Model vocabulary collecting using sticky notes; transfer to composition book

Read Chapter 3—whole group

Collect vocabulary—ongoing

Examine and practice reading strategies worksheet

Read to self—Chapter 4

Introduce timeline and begin comparing each story line

Small-group activities and reading—Chapter 4

Academic prompt—response to literature (RRJs)

Assign at-home reading—Chapter 5

Stage 3—Establish Learning Plan

Day 4:

Share interesting or unfamiliar vocabulary words/definitions

Read Chapter 6—whole group

Collect vocabulary—ongoing

Read to self—Chapter 7

Mental image worksheet

Small-group activities and reading—Chapter 7

Assign at-home reading—Chapter 8

Day 5:

Share interesting or unfamiliar vocabulary words/definitions

Read Chapter 9—whole group

Y-chart feeling brainstorm

Collect vocabulary—ongoing

Read to self—Chapter 10

Academic prompt—response to literature (RRJs)

Small-group activities and reading—Chapter 10

Assign at-home reading—Chapter 11

Day 6:

Share interesting or unfamiliar vocabulary words/definitions

Read Chapter 12—whole group

Collect vocabulary—ongoing

Read to self—Chapter 13

Exercise on plot, character, setting, and theme

Small-group activities and reading—Chapter 13

Assign at-home reading—Chapter 14

Stage 3—Establish Learning Plan

Day 7:

Share interesting or unfamiliar vocabulary words/definitions

Read Chapter 15—whole group

Collect vocabulary—ongoing

Read to self—Chapter 16

Academic prompt—response to literature (RRJs)

Small-group activities and reading—Chapter 16

Assign at-home reading—Chapter 17

Day 8:

Share interesting or unfamiliar vocabulary words/definitions

Read Chapter 18—whole group

Review prediction posters (from day 1)

Academic prompt—response to literature (RRJs)

Day 9:

Read David and Goliath from the Bible—1 Samuel 17

Watch YouTube video clip: "The Bible—David and Goliath" (https://www.youtube.com/watch?v=fdyFGUh_Kpo&t=7s)

Compare and contrast Salva and David—whole group

Day 10:

Class discussion—What is an obituary? Find one using local newspaper exercise.

Introduce obituaries—elements of an obituary

Search and find exercise—local newspaper, "What is an obituary?" checklist

Read Martin Luther King's obituary—find elements of an obituary using "Write an Obituary" planner

Performance Task—Write "Salva's Obituary" using the planner; gather elements of Salva's life via text, draft, revise, edit, publish

Other Ideas:

Read picture book *Rosa* by Nikki Giovanni

Revisit "The Columbian" article on Diana Golden, Holocaust survivor (sample obituary)

UbD and Differentiation

The *T* in WHERETO refers to tailoring lessons to the needs of the students. Today's popular term for this area is differentiation. Some people see differentiation as individualized instruction, but it is an unreasonable expectation for teachers to create individualized lessons for all their students in each of the subject areas in elementary, or for the substantial numbers of students that secondary teachers are responsible for.

A leading differentiation expert, Dr. Carol Ann Tomlinson, has stated that a key premise foundation of differentiation is to provide all students access to a high-quality curriculum that includes ideas and skills valued by experts in a field and that provides a framework for the diversity of learners in today's classrooms.

Teachers develop many skills over time, and differentiation could be the most complex and challenging of all. This is a skill that can be learned but does require thoughtful and intentional planning to implement effectively.

In 2006, Tomlinson and McTighe wrote *Integrating Differentiated Instruction and Understanding by Design*. UbD is the curriculum design framework, and differentiation is an instructional design tool. The following quote expresses the relationship between UbD and differentiation.

> The convergence of the two models is useful for addressing two of the greatest contemporary challenges for educators–crafting powerful curriculum in a standards-dominated era and ensuring academic success for the full spectrum of learners . . . UbD and differentiated instruction are not only mutually supportive of one another but, in fact, 'need' one another.[2]

In the book, they outlined five elements required for differentiation to occur:

- supportive learning environment
- continual assessment
- high-quality curriculum
- respectful tasks
- flexible grouping

---

2. Tomlinson and McTighe, *Integrating*, 2.

TAILORING & DIFFERENTIATION

TAILORING ALLOWS FOR "OWNERSHIP OF YOUR STUDENTS...A KEY PREMISE TO DIFFERENTIATED INSTRUCTION."
– TOMLINSON

STAGE ONE
DESIRED RESULTS

ESTABLISHED GOALS
What relevant goals will this design address? (content standards, course or program objectives, learning outcomes)

UNDERSTANDINGS
What are the big ideas? What specific understandings about them are desired? What misunderstandings are predictable?

ESSENTIAL QUESTIONS
What provocative questions will foster inquiry, understanding, and transfer of learning?

STUDENTS WILL KNOW / BE ABLE TO
What key knowledge and skills will students acquire as a result of this unit? What should they eventually be able to do as a result of this knowledge and skill?

STAGE TWO
ASSESSMENT EVIDENCE

PERFORMANCE TASKS
Through what authentic performance tasks will students demonstrate the desired understandings?
By what criteria will "performances of understanding" be judged?

OTHER EVIDENCE
Through what other evidence will students demonstrate achievement of the desired results? (e.g. quizzes, tests, academic prompts, observation, homework, journals) How will students reflect upon and self-assess their learning?

STAGE THREE
LEARNING PLAN

LEARNING ACTIVITIES
What learning experiences and instruction will enable students to achieve the desired results?
How will the design...

W Help the students know **WHERE** the unit is going and **WHAT** is expected? Help the teacher know **WHERE** the students are coming from (prior knowledge, interests)?

H **HOOK** all students and **HOLD** their interest?

E **EQUIP** students, help them **EXPERIENCE** the key ideas, and **EXPLORE** the issues?

R Provide opportunities to **RETHINK** and **REVISE** their understandings at work?

E Allow students to **EVALUATE** their work and its implications?

T Be **TAILORED** (personalized) to different needs, interests, and abilities of learners?

O Be **ORGANIZED** to maximize initial and sustained engagement as well?

	SHOULD NOT BE DIFFERENTIATED
	MAY BE DIFFERENTIATED
	SHOULD BE DIFFERENTIATED

Based on data from Carol Ann Tomlinson & Jay McTighe, *Integrating Differentiated Instruction and Understanding by Design*, ASCD, 2006, p. 36.

These authors provided suggestions for where UbD and differentiation best intersect. When it comes to tailoring the instruction, each stage of Understanding by Design has a different relationship with differentiation.

Considering the differences in students within a classroom is foundational to implementing differentiated instruction, because those differences are significant. Biologically, students differ in gender, development, and abilities. Students have different interests and learning preferences. Economic status, race, culture, support systems, language, and experience all impact student readiness to learn. Students' self-image, motivation, temperament, interpersonal skills, adult models, and trust play into their students' willingness to engage in the classroom.

Being cognizant that the difficulty level of the content needs to be both challenging and achievable is important. When work is too challenging, students do not engage in the learning; when content is too easy, students become uninterested.

Students who struggle in classrooms often need reading support and vocabulary building. They may need extra support to fill in gaps in their knowledge and skills. Advanced learners sometimes fail to develop coping skills because they are used to being successful without much effort, or they become perfectionists. They can possibly become mentally lazy.

From a Christian school perspective, it is important to be reminded that we are all uniquely made. Psalm 139:14 (NIV) states, "I praise you because I am fearfully and wonderfully made; your works are wonderful, I know that full well." Interestingly, brain research has discovered that every brain is unique. Each person is made in God's image and is special in God's kingdom. That makes every student significant.

Therefore, expecting all students to be able to achieve the school's mission-related outcomes requires staff to include instructional practices that benefit all students. There are dozens of books on differentiation in the classroom, many available webinars, and whole conferences on this topic. Making differentiation a topic for staff to deeply explore and implement over time is a worthy consideration.

Tomlinson identified seven classroom elements to consider when differentiating lesson design to increase students' chances for success:

- time
- space
- resources

- student groupings
- teaching strategies
- learning strategies
- teacher partnerships

Within each of these areas, there are a variety of options for teachers to consider when planning lessons for Stage 3.

Also, deciding on which students should enroll and be effectively served is an ongoing challenge in a Christian school. When differentiation becomes embedded into a Christian school's instructional practice, it not only better serves the existing students' learning, but also may open opportunities to serve students who in the past were not able to enroll and be successful because of the school's instructional practices.

The Impact of Technology on Instruction

We are living in a time where significant technological advances are changing the world around us. Considering how technology fits into today's instructional program is a hot topic in educational circles. Currently, there is certainly no consensus on what changes need to be made, although there are many interesting approaches being taken, especially among charter schools. Christian schools are faced with deciding not only what technology to employ but also, pedagogically, how to best use technology to enhance student learning.

Looking back over history, we know that the invention of the Gutenberg printing press in 1439 opened the world to a whole new way to transmit knowledge (in particular the Bible). Over the following centuries, access to information increased dramatically for the masses. In America, since the mid-1800s when education went from a privilege to a right, educators have been the keepers of knowledge and have done their best to educate the majority of youth.

In the last twenty years, the development and availability of the World Wide Web has changed access to information and knowledge. In fact, the impact that technology is having may be more dramatic than most of us realize. There is no area of life that is not being significantly impacted by technology today, and educators may be facing a revolution that they have yet to fully grasp. Most educators, Christian or not, started in this profession at a time when they were solely responsible for disseminating knowledge. They now may be entering a time when they no longer will be serving in this same role, because knowledge is no longer held by few people.

Technology has opened access to content, knowledge, and teachers to anyone. Learning is no longer required to be done from 8:00 a.m. to 3:00 p.m. Students can readily explore interests and passions outside the walls of the traditional school. Students can communicate in real time with others from anywhere in the world, create and publish work, and determine their own learning.

> The cure for boredom is curiosity. There is no cure for curiosity.
>
> —DOROTHY PARKER

Without question, technology is an integral part of life for today's students. Students today have grown up in a world where mobile computers, cell phones with browsers, and other personal digital devices are common tools. Instant messaging, social media, blogs, and tweets are common modes of self-expression. Students today desire to learn in an environment that mirrors their lives and their futures—one that seamlessly integrates today's digital tools, accommodates a mobile lifestyle, and encourages collaboration and teamwork in physical and virtual spaces.

An interesting twist is that current teachers are considered technology immigrants while children are technology natives. This creates a perplexing dilemma in schools, where students often know more about the use of technology (especially social media) than the adults. Often students are asked to turn off their "normal" world of being engaged with technology and drop into an adult context disconnected from the platform of instant communication and access to nearly unlimited information.

Students need to acquire twenty-first century skills such as innovation and creativity, critical thinking and problem solving, and information and media literacy, along with character traits of self-direction, adaptability, and accountability. Technology can be an asset in this quest. So how should a school proceed with technology to both harness student motivation and achieve its mission?

UbD and Technology

A foundational principle when considering the use of technology in an instructional program is that the focus should be on student learning and not
on the technology itself. How technology can be used as a tool to further
learning should be the primary concern. The use of technology is not the
end goal. Technology is typically used in schools as a new way to do old
things. However, technology's greatest asset is that it enables students to do
powerful new things that they couldn't do before.

A productive approach for schools is to first spend time developing a
mission-focused curriculum, then consider how technology can support
the instructional program. For example, if a desired outcome of a Christian
school is for students to be effective and critical thinkers, then a key question would be "How could technology cultivate critical thinking during the
instructional process?" Because of the push for integration of technology
into the classroom, often schools introduce a variety of technology tools
(SMART boards, document cameras, iPads, Chromebooks, laptops, LCD
screens, mobile furniture, etc.) into classrooms without having a clear emphasis for their use or with proper training for teachers. The result can be
unfocused technology-based activities or the tools not being used at all.

Using the Understanding by Design framework for planning curriculum provides schools with clear, instructional, mission-driven outcomes.
For a Christian school, this provides staff a means to carefully consider
what technology would best serve them. The traditional direct instruction
using whiteboards and textbooks is still an essential component for educating students. However, there is no question—in order to engage young
people who are growing up with technology in a cyberworld, teachers must
incorporate a greater level of technology into schools. By taking advantage
of these resources and teaching their effective and appropriate use, teachers
are helping to ensure students will be best prepared to grasp new technological trends and utilize them to their fullest advantage in a twenty-first
century world. Rethinking traditional curriculum and instructional methods because of the impact that technology is having on education is in the
best interest of today's student.

The implementation of instructional technology should be done under the umbrella of a much larger undertaking of improving teacher unit
design practices and schoolwide curriculum revision. Embracing the use
of technology, securing the tools, and having the opportunity to implement
instructional strategies to cultivate student learning are critical elements in

a school improvement plan. Teachers will become more than just information experts but also facilitators and collaborators of learning—leveraging the power of students, seeking new knowledge alongside students, and modeling lifelong learning. Students can use digital tools and applications that access information and reference materials, calculate or record data, and create products that meet a school's mission-related outcomes.

In the end, the desire is to prepare students to be community members who follow Jesus Christ and serve others. Preparing students with desirable skills and characteristics (strong work ethic; collaboration; spiritual and social responsibility; critical thinking and problem solving; creativity and innovation) is an admirable objective. The inclusion of instructional technology tools is a significant component of the educational program.

Staff Development and Technology

Placing technology tools into a classroom does not ensure that they will be used effectively. Teachers and school leaders will need to participate in professional development to rethink curriculum and instructional practices that best harness the power of technology to increase student learning. Staff will need both instruction and consistent support on the use of hardware and software tools. Classroom instruction time is a precious commodity. Teachers will not consistently engage students in use of the technology in the classroom without the equipment working in a dependable manner.

In addition, professional development activities on instructional strategies for teachers are critical. For example, one model for training teachers on the use of technology is SAMR. This model was popularized by Dr. Ruben Puentedura, a member of the Maine Learning Technology Initiative and founder and president of Hippasus. SAMR provides a structure for teachers to design, develop, and infuse digital learning experiences that utilize technology.

The acronym SAMR represents

- Substitution: The technology acts as a direct substitute, with no functional change.

- Augmentation: The technology allows for significant task redesign.

- Modification: The technology acts as a direct substitute, with functional improvement.

- Redefinition: The technology allows for creation of new tasks, previously inconceivable.

When first implementing technology, teachers often use substitution or modification methods. When viewing technology use through the SAMR model, teachers are encouraged to use technology in all four approaches.

Teachers are generally more than willing to engage in new and creative strategies when they can see models of success. The role of an instructional coach can be a key to the success. An instructional coach works with teachers to ensure that their lessons and projects are about rigorous, relevant curriculum rather than about the technology.

Key Chapter Takeaways

✓ Include strategies that brain research has revealed improve the chances for long-term memory and transfer when planning daily lessons for a unit.

✓ Wiggins and McTighe have devised several tools to remind teachers of productive strategies and practices for increasing student learning.

✓ Differentiation is an indispensable element of planning an Understanding by Design framework unit.

✓ Differentiation is a high-level skill that teachers typically develop over time, and it is a topic that is worthy of regular consideration for staff development.

✓ Technology is making significant changes in our world, and considering how best to use technology in a Christian school is an important consideration.

✓ The use of technology is not the end goal, but schools should view the use of technology as a tool to achieve their mission and outcomes.

✓ Staff development is critical for staff when new technology is implemented.

Concluding Thoughts

The final task in planning a UbD unit is to check for alignment of the three stages. One way to complete this final task is for teachers to ask themselves these three questions:

- Do the planned lessons end up providing evidence of the students' understanding of the big ideas, enduring understandings, knowledge, and skills?

- Does the valid and reliable evidence generated over the course of the unit reveal students' understanding of the big idea and acquisition of knowledge and skills?

- What is the connection in this unit to the school's mission and related desired student outcomes?

Being thoughtful and careful in development of the learning plan pays great dividends in student learning.

Educator Interview

Q: You have been a technology teacher in a K–8 Christian school for more than fifteen years. The school has embraced Understanding by Design (UbD). What were some of the shifts in thinking that were made during this process of change?

Technology Teacher

DARIUS MOVAFAGIAN

Bio

K–8 Technology Teacher
Technology Specialist

BA, Art/Multimedia,
    California State Hayward
MA, Teaching, City
    University of Seattle

A: For some reason, our staff took a while to fully embrace the UbD model. Most agreed that it had merits, but not everyone was willing to jump in with both feet. Administrators were patient. They explained that this was a multiyear plan and continued to follow up with training and support. Eventually, classrooms were outfitted with furniture that was mobile and easily reconfigured for student collaboration and small groupings. When technology was introduced to the classrooms, student engagement really took off. Teachers began to see that UbD was more a way of thinking and planning and not just another way of doing school. One of the things that we are doing today are PLCs (Professional Learning Community.) Teachers meet once a month solely focused on UbD, to write and review units. It has become part of the fabric of the school.

Q: As a technology teacher, how do you support teachers in implementing the UbD framework and integrating technology into instruction? How do UbD and technology interconnect?

A: When teaching with technology, it should be seamless. Any problems with infrastructure, software, or hardware are going to frustrate all involved and lead the teacher to not trust that their tools will work. The IT/tech departments work very hard to ensure that everything is performing at its best. With that in mind, I feel that we are always prioritizing professional development with teachers, both large and small groups, regarding things like how to best utilize classroom software, using their SMART boards, even learning Windows 10. The more teachers understand the tools at their disposal, the more confident they are at planning lessons involving technology. When they are willing to troubleshoot problems that may occur and not let small things derail their lesson, they are willing to take more risks and try new things. This opens the door to more choices when integrating technology with UbD. This leads to performance tasks or culminating projects with more diversity. Students are then more engaged, and they begin to own their learning.

I also plan with teachers in preparing students with the soft skills they may need for upcoming units. Depending on the time, I use about three to five class meetings to work with students on using Office to write essays in Word or make PowerPoint presentations. Some classes learn how to use cameras or iPads for green screen projects or stop motion. We learn how to use camcorders and editing software for video projects. The main focus is trying to connect the technology and performance task back to learning and understanding. Students like the opportunity to share what they know using technology.

Q: Your school has implemented student performance tasks and individual student portfolios to collect evidence on student understanding. How have these practices impacted teachers and students? Is there any relationship between this evidence and the school's mission?

A: I feel student portfolios impact the students because they see that their work matters. I hope they make the connection that they are responsible for their learning. If so, it is reflected in the quality of their performance task. For teachers, the performance task engages the student and has helped develop a connection to learning that the students can articulate during their student-led conference. Everything is connected and tied together. The required elements of the portfolio are tied directly to the school's priority learning results. These learning results are a reflection of the school's mission.

Q: What advice would you have for teachers first starting out when planning units using the UbD framework and integrating technology?

A: I would suggest reaching out to your school's library/media specialist or your district's technology coach for suggestions on integrating appropriate technology for your units. Another resource is to join or create a local PLC (Professional Learning Community). Start with other staff at your school, then your district. Connecting with other educators is a great way to share knowledge and get feedback on your successes or disappointments. It takes a bit of time to create good units. Both writing and refining units occur over time. It's important to get timely and constructive feedback and support.

6

Systemic Thinking

Established systems are inherently hostile to change.

—NEWT GINGRICH

A bad system will beat a good person every time.

—W. EDWARDS DEMING

LONG-TERM STRATEGIC THINKING ALLOWS staff to focus their limited time and energy on productive actions that concentrate on the vision and goals of the mission. Peter M. Senge argues that systemic thinking is invaluable in the change process.[1] Thinking systemically has its place in Christian education.

Helping teachers to establish mission-driven units of instruction is not sufficient to achieve the full measure of results for the desired mission-based student outcomes. Every school, including Christian schools, has numerous systems in place. They exist based on past practices and are often assumed to be the best way to function. Taking time to look closely at the various aspects of a school's organization is not done often. Even during the intermittent accreditation process, it is usually only reported on rather than analyzed. Occasionally, an issue will arise that causes one area of the school to be examined and changes made, but rarely does the school's leadership

1. Senge, *The Fifth Discipline*.

and staff take time for systemic analysis of all the components that affect the instructional program.

> Wisdom is the knowledge of the nature of things, the reasons
> behind what happens. Someone has described wisdom
> as the right use of knowledge. It is how to use situations
> in such a way that things work out right.
>
> —RAY STEDMAN

Christian school leaders have the benefit of receiving direction from the Holy Spirit and exercising godly wisdom in their decision-making. The school board members, administrators, and teacher leaders are responsible for setting the direction of their schools through its mission and vision. The school's administration and teacher leaders have the privilege of operationalizing this course. Therefore, it would seem logical to periodically pause and analyze the school's systems in relation to the instructional program and then add to their existing strategic plan (which usually focuses on finances and facilities) a section on improving the instructional program.

Christian schools also have another decided advantage over public school systems in that they are usually much smaller organizations. Most public schools are part of districtwide systems, and making significant change lies somewhere between very difficult and impossible. There are just too many layers of approval for anything to get done and many voices (community groups, school board, unions, parent groups, etc.) pulling for their specific agendas to get heard and approved. The close-knit nature and smaller size of Christian schools is an asset in conducting a system analysis and making substantive improvements.

On the flip side, Christian schools are sometimes prone to maintain the status quo. In Gene Frost's book *Learning from the Best: Growing Greatness that Endures in the Christian School,* he found that one of the problems endangering Christian schools is the stubborn determination to perpetuate the status quo, rather than using inspiration to build the future by being creative and innovative while staying true to core Christian beliefs.

So what should a Christian school's leadership evaluate with regards to the instructional program? Wiggins and McTighe recognized that there was more to changing the culture of schools than just improving teachers' instructional design. They wrote a book, *Schooling by Design,* which addresses this issue and which can certainly be applied to Christian schools. This book provides an extension of Understanding by Design (starting with the end in mind). It includes a set of practical strategies and structures to realize a school's mission.

BACKWARD DESIGN FOR SCHOOL IMPROVEMENT

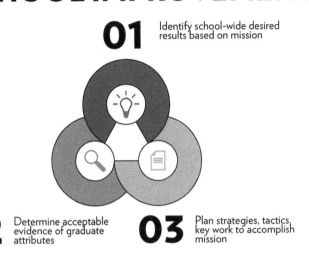

01 Identify school-wide desired results based on mission

02 Determine acceptable evidence of graduate attributes

03 Plan strategies, tactics, key work to accomplish mission

Based on data from Jay McTighe and Grant Wiggins, *Schooling by Design*, 2007.

Wiggins and McTighe outlined six major areas for the school's leadership to analyze and align to their mission and vision:

- mission and philosophy
- learning principles
- curriculum and assessment systems
- instructional programs and practices
- personnel: hiring, appraisal, and development
- policies, structures, governance, and resources

As noted in Chapter 1, most people view the purpose of schools as intellectual, political, economic, or social. Although each of these purposes has value, the key mission of Christian schools is to help students grow spiritually and prepare them to impact the world for Christ. A Christian school's most important work is to orchestrate the organization's curriculum, instruction, and assessment program; personnel and resources; and policies, structures, and procedures to achieve that mission.

Mission and Philosophy

A mission is a commitment to a few priority results, from which some pedagogical implications logically follow. From a Christian perspective, the primary purpose of a Christian school is the spiritual development of students. Based on the school's mission, there are usually several other outcomes that schools have selected as their highest priorities. As noted in Chapter 3, taking the time to be clear on the school's primary outcomes is without question foundational.

In *Managing the Nonprofit Organization: Principles and Practices*, Peter Drucker wrote:

> The most common question asked of me by nonprofit executives is: What are the qualities of a leader? The question seems to assume that leadership is something you can learn in a charm school . . . What matters is not the leader's charisma. What matters is the leader's mission. Therefore, the first job of the leaders is to think through and define the mission of the institution . . . The task of the nonprofit manager is to try to convert the mission statement into specifics.[2]

Without a commitment to a mission, a purposeful school does not exist; staff are just a group of independent teacher contractors connected by a common parking lot.

As an example, if one of the school's student outcomes is that students have effective relationships and are good communicators, then the implication is that the school's curriculum include regular opportunities for students to write and speak in authentic settings.

Learning Principles

The second foundational area is the school's learning principles. Developing a set of principles of learning that guide instructional program decisions and strategies is an additional step a school should take to sustain its

2. Drucker, *Managing the Nonprofit Organization*, 3.

mission. These principles should be generated based on current educational brain research and best practices.

This will require time for staff to read about current education topics and conduct discussions about their beliefs. Having a clear picture of what current brain research has revealed about how the brain learns best and what have been found to be best practices within education is an important foundational step.

Some teachers' beliefs come from their past practices and comfort level and are not always rooted in what is now known about quality teaching and learning. If a school is approaching the development of its curriculum around the UbD framework, then some traditionally held ideas will be challenged.

Consider these in the process: Do the principles support teaching for understanding and transfer? Are the learning principles consistent with the school's mission? Are metacognitive activities and formative assessments considered vital? How important is it to embed differentiation into the instructional program? What types of assessment are valued system-wide?

Coming to a consensus on what are believed to be the most important learning principles provides a set of standards for professionalism and a platform for discussion about the school's curriculum, instruction, and assessment practices along with the school's personnel, policy, governance, and resources. Once this is completed, then individual teacher's personal opinions should no longer be the basis for deliberations about the instructional program.

In addition, when new staff are hired and trained, the learning principles can be used as a basis for setting expectations for what instruction is to look like at the school. Some schools even post on their web page their agreed-upon learning principles. This gives potential new administrators and teachers insight into what is important in the school, and it also can affect possible new families in considering the school for enrollment for their child.

Read the two examples from Christian schools that have developed a set of learning principles.

Example #1

1. Learners will be encouraged to *set godly standards and excellence goals* for developing their gifts, talents, and passions.

2. Learning involves language and, likewise, language influences learning. Language pedagogies will focus on the interpretation and *construction of meaning* as learners collaborate and engage at a personal and corporate level.

3. Learners will engage in learning from a *contextual relationship* that builds on prior knowledge, through personal beliefs, prejudices, and fears.

4. Learning requires *time* and is neither instantaneous nor static. For significant learning to occur, learners need to revisit ideas, ponder them, try them out, and use them repeatedly.

5. *Meaning and relevancy* is vital to learning, teaching, and assessing. In order for meaning to be realized, it is important to provide regular opportunities for students to see value in what they are asked to learn and how it relates to prior and future learning.

6. To maximize learning, learners need multiple opportunities to practice in risk-free environments. Learners shall receive regular and specific *feedback* related to progress against standards with timely opportunities to utilize feedback and improve.

7. *Integration of biblical foundational truths* shall be presented regularly. Learners will investigate evidences that clearly demonstrate the authority, authenticity, and accuracy of the Scriptures, particularly in light of religious, scientific, and cultural norms conflicting with a biblical worldview.

8. In order to best engage students, academic lessons are based on *high-interest topics* that engage and motivate the student or that have functional learning benefits that the student values and can apply in his or her own life.

Example #2

1. The goal of learning is to develop *wisdom and understanding* and to be able to apply knowledge in a variety of contexts. "When I was a child, I spoke and thought and reasoned as a child" (1 Corinthians 13:11 NLT).

2. The most worthwhile and engaging learning is that which constantly points back to the greater *truths of God's design* while connecting to the life of the student.

3. Learning is a *multisensory, active process* requiring time, reflection, and revisitation.

4. Assessment in the learning process should be done by both the student and teacher and align with *specific goals*.

5. Learning should happen in a *safe environment* that encourages both growth and risk.

6. In order for students to continue to learn and grow, the entire school community of faculty and staff must be committed to learning and growing themselves through *continual professional development*.

7. All students have God-given gifts and abilities to be discovered through the learning process, and *strong relationships between staff and students* allow for better discovery of those talents.

Each statement has implications regarding the curriculum, instruction, and/or assessments in the instructional program. In some cases, they may even have consequences for other areas of the school (hiring, policies, schedules, student reporting systems, calendars).

For example, if a school believes that it takes time for meaning to be constructed, then it may require the school to look at the amount of content that is being covered. Teachers often are trying to push through a long list of standards and/or trying to cover as much of a textbook as possible in the time allotted. Instead, teachers could identify the most important content to be covered and then chart a course of action.

The school's mission and its principles of learning are the foundation for the rest of the school's systems. When these two elements are clearly defined and used as primary guides for the school's other systems, there is a purposeful cohesiveness about the school. The graphic from *Schooling by Design* is a visual representation of the six major areas for systemic analysis.

POLICIES, PROCEDURES, RESOURCE ALLOCATION & GOVERNANCE

HUMAN RESOURCES, HIRING, APPRAISAL & STAFF DEVELOPMENT

LEARNING OPPORTUNITIES & PEDAGOGICAL PRACTICES

VERTICALLY-ALIGNED CURRICULUM & ASSESSMENT SYSTEM

MISSION, VISION & TRANSFER GOALS

LEARNING PRINCIPLES

APPLYING STRATEGIC PRINCIPLES & USING BACKWARD DESIGN

SCHOOLING BY DESIGN AREAS FOR SYSTEMIC ANALYSIS

Based on data from Jay McTighe, 2019.

Curricular Systems

As noted in Chapter 3, Robert Marzano has concluded that a "guaranteed and viable curriculum is the number-one school-level factor impacting student achievement." The curriculum of a school is the course of study that the school has decided is most important for their students to study. With the knowledge explosion that is going on in the world and the ready access to knowledge, it is especially important today to carefully consider what a school wants the students to know and understand.

In a school using the Understanding by Design framework, the curriculum should highlight understanding and transfer of learning and should be derived from the mission of the school. In *Schooling by Design*, Wiggins and McTighe outline ten components of a well-developed curriculum framework:

1. Mission-related accomplishments and curricular philosophy

2. Understandings and essential questions derived from the mission

3. K–12 curriculum mapping

4. Cornerstone assessments and collections of evidence

5. Analytic and longitudinal rubrics

6. Anchors

7. Suggested learning activities, teaching strategies, and resources

8. Diagnostic and formative assessments

9. Suggestions for differentiation

10. Troubleshooting guide[3]

Schooling by Design provides an in-depth look at each element. To undertake developing a complete curriculum framework in this manner is a multiyear project. The end result is a school with a sophisticated network of tools that support a high-quality instructional program that will serve the school well for many years.

The curriculum framework documents can be kept electronically so that they are readily available to all staff. Rather than being a curriculum etched in stone, some aspects become more organic in nature, with teachers revising and adding information. Over time, the mission and

---

3. Wiggins and McTighe, *Schooling by Design*, 60.

learning principles remain constant. Changes to the curriculum maps, cornerstone assessments, and longitudinal rubrics can occur using a collaborative process. This work allows for changes in administrators and teachers but keeps the heart of the school focused on the mission, and the school remains stable.

Developing curriculum maps has been a common practice in education for decades, and they typically have been a list of knowledge and skill-based standards. In a school using the Understanding by Design framework, the curriculum maps would need to include the big ideas, enduring understandings, and essential questions, along with the related knowledge and skills.

Once teachers understand the Understanding by Design framework, then they can step back and consider their curriculum maps. This work is most effectively done collaboratively with other teachers. It is usually an iterative process. Initially, grade-level or subject-specific teachers suggest the big ideas for the year. Then, these are charted for everyone to see. Reviewing these with the mission-related outcomes in mind is useful at this point. Ask questions like these:

- For elementary: Where does my grade-level curriculum support the key mission-related outcomes?

- For secondary: Where in my subject-level curriculum are the key mission-related outcomes taught?

Also, it is important to look at the big ideas and mission-related outcomes that are being taught over the span of school years (K–5, K–8, or K–12) to make sure they are being consistently addressed.

For example, if spiritual development of students is primary, where does biblical integration occur in each subject? Or if students are to become servant leaders, where in the curriculum are biblical servanthood and leadership taught? Do these happen consistently and logically over the course of a student's schooling?

If the school desires students to become lifelong learners, then where in the curriculum does the school allow for student choice to pursue a topic that they are curious about?

If a school has five mission-related outcomes (e.g., students who are growing spiritually, are productive thinkers, are involved in effective action, have effective relationships, and are lifelong learners), then it would be valuable to chart when each of these is intentionally addressed in units of instruction with performance tasks aimed at collecting evidence of understanding. This would be a way to increase fidelity in being a mission-based school.

Lastly, there are a variety of electronic platforms for curriculum mapping. The important thing is to choose a consistent format for all grade levels and subject areas that has options for including big ideas, enduring understandings, essential questions, knowledge, and skills. A common format is useful when it comes to cross-curricular or cross-grade-level discussions and peer review work.

I have provided two examples of what a curriculum map could look like. The ELA grade 8 example curriculum map comes from a school in which leadership is a mission-related outcome. It does not include the writing, speaking and listening, and language strands information.

English-Language Arts—Grade 8

Big Idea/Theme—Leadership

Enduring Understandings	Essential Questions	Strand	Skills and Knowledge
God can make a leader out of the least of us. Service is the foundation of leadership. A good leader must also be a good follower. Leadership often means doing the hard thing. Experiencing various opportunities in life can give insight into good decisions as a leader.	What makes a good leader? Is being a servant being a leader? Why would someone want to be a leader? Do age and experience impact leadership?	*Reading Literature*	*Craft and Structure* Determine the meaning of words and phrases as they are used in a text, including figurative and connotative meanings; analyze the impact of specific word choices on meaning and tone, including analogies or allusions to other texts. Analyze how differences in the points of view of the characters and the audience or reader (e.g., created through the use of dramatic irony) create such effects as suspense or humor. *Range of Reading and Level of Text Complexity* By the end of the year, read and comprehend literature, including stories, dramas, and poems, at the high end of grades 6–8 text complexity band, independently and proficiently.
		Reading Information Text	*Craft and Structure* Analyze in detail the structure of a specific paragraph in a text, including the role of particular sentences in developing and refining a key concept. *Integration of Knowledge and Ideas* Analyze a case in which two or more texts provide conflicting information on the same topic, and identify where the texts disagree on matters of fact or interpretation.

Mathematics—Grade 2

Big Idea/Theme—Geometry

Enduring Understandings	Essential Questions	Standard	Skills and Knowledge
Students will understand that geometric figures are all around us in various forms. Students will understand that angles, vertices, faces, sides, and edges are all attributes of two- and three-dimensional figures. Students will understand that fractions are an integral part of our daily life and an important tool in solving problems. Students will understand that to reason mathematically means to think abstractly and quantitatively.	Did God use geometric figures when he created the world? Where can we find geometric figures in the world around us? Why is it important to be able to identify and describe geometric figures? How do we use the following terms: angle, vertex, face, side, and edge to describe geometric figures? How do we apply the use of fractions in everyday life? Can we use geometric figures to solve problems?	*Reason with shapes and their attributes*	Recognize and draw shapes having specified attributes, such as a given number of angles or a given number of equal faces. Identify triangles, quadrilaterals, pentagons, hexagons, and cubes. Partition a rectangle into rows and columns of same-size squares and count to find the total number of them. Partition circles and rectangles into two, three, or four equal shares, describe the shares using the words halves, thirds, half of, a third of, etc., and describe the whole as two halves, three thirds, four fourths. Recognize that equal shares of identical wholes need not have the same shape.

Once curriculum maps are established, then the selection of instructional materials can be approached thoughtfully. Teachers are not looking for a single-solution textbook for each subject area or course of study; instead, they are looking for a set of materials that best supports the units of instruction driven by the curriculum map.

Textbooks are looked at as one of several resources to use when teaching the unit of instruction. In some cases, there may be no single text at all, but rather an array of instructional materials. For example, in upper-grade-level English-Language Arts or Humanities courses, it may be better to implement a variety of literature and/or history books along with some grammar and vocabulary materials. Or in a Bible class, using the Scriptures along with some biblically based authors could be a more productive option. The goal in the end would be to find the materials that best support the big ideas, enduring understandings, essential questions, skills, and knowledge that are taught in the course.

In David I. Smith's book *On Christian Teaching*, he encourages teachers to look for the cultural biases in textbooks. Being a foreign language teacher, he describes a textbook that he had used that consistently had dialogues that focused on travel, food, hobbies, clothing, and holiday customs. These things in themselves are not bad, but matters like people praying, giving sacrificially of their time and resources, facing difficult choices, acts of compassion, school and work relationships, suffering, protests, or injustices were never addressed. As Christian school teachers, if all that is presented to students during a course is self-oriented content, it seems that an opportunity is missed. He argues that the primary reason for students to take a world language is that people from other countries are our neighbors (not just for college entrance or employment). The Scriptures are clear on the Christian's responsibility to love their neighbor (Matthew 22:37–39).

Smith gives other examples: physical education—competition (win at all cost) vs. love within teamwork; science—just teaching the Christian perspective on controversial issues or including discussions about virtues needed to be a good scientist. There are implications for Christian school educators for every content area to uncover the inherent biases in their subject area and to consider how they might reshape practices.

Assessment Systems

The goal of a school's assessment system is to collect evidence that reveals the curriculum is achieving the desired mission-based results. A school should cultivate the use of a range of assessments that give a broader picture of how it is achieving its mission rather than only using standardized test results, honor roll, grade point average (GPA), graduation rates, college acceptance numbers, attendance, and discipline.

Collecting and reporting traditional data still has its value. Standardized test scores, SAT, ACT, and AP scores are usually the data that Christian schools use to compare how their students are performing related to other schools. If the above list is the sole data used in a Christian school, then the message given is that knowledge and skills are most important.

Collecting other types of evidence allows a school to see other aspects of their students' development. Assessments such as portfolios, student-led conferences, student exhibitions, writing assessments, and school-developed cornerstone performance tasks can provide evidence of student understanding of bigger ideas, enduring understandings, and character development.

When a school has a balanced assessment system, the message given to students and their families is that the school values more than just a student's GPA or acquisition of knowledge and skills.

Portfolios

Portfolios are a nontraditional means of assessment that allow for students to showcase their strengths in other areas in addition to memorization of knowledge and skill retention. A portfolio assessment offers the opportunity to observe students in a broader context: understanding of complex questions, taking risks, developing creative solutions, and learning to make judgments about their own performances.

> A portfolio is a purposeful collection of student work that exhibits to the students and/or others the student's efforts, progress, or achievement in a given area. This collection must include: student participation in the selection; the criteria for selection; the criteria for judging merit; and evidence of self-reflection or self-assessment.[4]

A portfolio allows each student the opportunity to demonstrate growth spiritually and academically and to engage in self-reflection and self-evaluation. A portfolio is an excellent tool to reveal student growth, progress, and depth of understanding.

Components of a portfolio can include carefully chosen pieces of student work and self-assessment/self-reflections. Content of individual portfolios will vary. School-developed guidelines provide students with specific criteria for the work placed in the portfolio that reveals evidence of student understanding of the school's mission-related outcomes. A portfolio is a meaningful way for students to reflect on their learning experiences and a way for the school staff to look at student learning. The student artifacts should be authentic class assessments or performance tasks that are from regular class work.

4. Lankes, "Electronic Portfolios," 2.

There are benefits in using student portfolios, for both students and parents, because portfolios provide

- students and parents with an indication of spiritual growth and academic progress along with depth of understanding on complex issues; and

- students with an opportunity to reflectively analyze effective thinking processes (metacognition).

There are also benefits for school site staff:

- Portfolios provide teachers and site administrators with summative student performance data that can assist in guiding instruction and the allocation of resources to support student learning.

- For teachers and administrators, the use of portfolios validates and encourages the rich curriculum, instruction, and assessment practices that focus on student understanding.

When students select their evidence, it should include and reflect a range of work from different classes and subjects. In addition, students should generate a reflection for each artifact submitted. If a student is engaged in a personally significant activity outside of school, the teacher can encourage the submittal of evidence that fits the portfolio guidelines.

Portfolios can be used in a variety of ways within a school. This can range from internal use in a student's class to a requirement for graduation. Using a rubric, portfolios can be evaluated by students, teachers, and/or community members. Regardless of how the portfolios are used, it is important to keep in mind that portfolios are a means to collect evidence and provide excellent feedback on student progress.

Today, electronic portfolios have made the collection and storage process much easier than the days of paper folders. For schools that have students keep portfolios annually, the electronic storage option allows students ready access to their work over many years. Students can look back over time and effortlessly see their growth and progress.

Students may need a list of ideas to consider. Using electronic portfolios opens up the option of submitting audio or video recordings.

Potential Artifacts for a Portfolio

Products	Performances
Advertisement	Audio File
Brochure	Demonstration
Drawing	Interview
Cartoon	Play
Data Display and/or Graph	Newscast
Diagram	Podcasts
Diary/Journal/Log	Skit
Diorama	Speech
Directions	Song
Editorial or Review	Video File
Exhibit	
Experiment	
Game	
Magazine or News Article	
Map	
Model	
Painting or Photograph	
Poem	
Poster	
Proposal or Plan	
PowerPoint	
Story or Script	
Website	
Writing—Informational/Explanatory, Argument-Opinion, Narrative	

Jay McTighe and Grant Wiggins,
Understanding by Design Workbook, ASCD, 2004, p. 174

Following is an example of portfolio guidelines for grade 8 from a Christian school that focused on the school's five priority outcomes. With each artifact, students completed the appropriate cover sheet. The purpose of the cover sheet is to help the reader of the portfolio understand the specific details of the expectations of the selection. The portfolios were presented by students to parents at the end of the school year, when student-led conferences were held.

Priority Outcome #1

Students will be growing spiritually and are individuals who

- have accepted and follow Jesus Christ as their Lord and Savior;
- have developed a respect and love for the Bible and understand that it is God's truth to mankind;
- understand they are uniquely created by God and continue to grow in character;
- show respect for and submission to God, family, and all other authority;
- have respect for their Christian and American heritage;
- understand the importance of the church and are responsible for evangelism; and
- understand their bodies are a temple of God which have developed a positive attitude, healthy eating, sleep habits, and physical routines.

For this part of the portfolio, each student will submit two artifacts that provide evidence that he or she is developing spiritually. Each artifact must reflect achievement in a different content area. Work samples will include

1. a reflection on the student's personal spiritual development during the current school year. It should address at least one of the above indicators for "Developing Spiritually;" and

2. a writing or speaking selection that addresses service to others.

Systemic Thinking

Priority Outcome #2

Students will be effective thinkers and are individuals who

- reason logically and depend on God for wisdom based on biblical standards;
- use diverse strategies and a biblical perspective in solving problems, making decisions, evaluating results, and applying knowledge to real-life situations;
- are creative and use critical thinking skills;
- read and comprehend a variety of materials; and
- articulately, effectively, and persuasively communicate orally, in writing, and artistically to a range of audiences in a variety of ways.

For this section, each student will submit two artifacts that provide evidence that the student is an effective thinker. Each selection must reflect achievement in a different content area. The work samples will include

1. a writing selection that addresses at least one of the critical thinking skills of the indicators above for "Effective Thinkers." Keep in mind that there are many critical thinking skills. Some critical thinking skills that are often taught in school are analyzing, interpreting, explaining, evaluating, inferring, clarifying, reasoning, predicting, comparing and contrasting, applying knowledge, exploring implications and consequences, identifying similarities and differences, and understanding different perspectives.

2. A speaking piece that addresses the effective oral communication skills indicator for effective thinkers.

Priority Outcome #3

Students will be involved in effective action resulting in notable accomplishments and are individuals who

- engage regularly in leadership opportunities with a problem-solving outlook;
- value time as a God-given commodity and manage projects with persistence;

- take initiative and work independently, which results in bringing honor to the Lord;

- are curious and are responsible for their own learning and actions;

- demonstrate integrity, responsibility, and perseverance as productive members of society; and

- understand the value of and are responsible to use material and knowledge resources for the glory of God.

For this section, each student will submit one artifact that provides evidence he or she has been involved in effective action.

1. Select a performance task that showed that the student took initiative and worked independently in a way that honored the Lord. If appropriate, include an explanation of how this performance task also addressed any other of the indicators for "Effective Action."

Priority Outcome #4

Students will have effective relationships and are individuals who

- demonstrate the principles of effective and godly communication;

- understand the importance of biblical ethics and actions in relationships;

- are accountable for his/her actions, treat everyone with respect, see issues from different perspectives because all are made in God's image;

- listen with understanding and empathy, follow instructions, and request clarification;

- are contributing members of their communities who are willing to serve others; and

- are able to work collaboratively in either face-to-face or through electronic media situations.

For this section, each student will submit one artifact that provides evidence that he/she can maintain effective relationships with other people.

1. Choose a writing selection or speaking piece that shows empathy or understanding of different perspectives. If possible, include examples that addressed any other of the indicators for "Effective Relationships."

Priority Outcome #5

Students will be lifelong learners who

- value learning as one of God's privileges and appreciate and love learning; and

- are responsible for continuing their own learning.

For this section, each student will submit one artifact that provides evidence that the student values and respects learning.

1. Choose a reading selection about a topic that the student is interested in or has a passion about and could possibly continue to pursue in the future. If possible, reveal to the reader other skills and/or attitudes of a "Lifelong Learner."

Just like rubrics that are used with performance tasks, rubrics for student portfolios should have clear and appropriate criteria that specify what we should look for. The sample shows what a rubric could look like for student self-evaluation or teacher evaluation.

Criteria	Exemplary Achievement	Proficient Achievement	Developing Achievement	Emerging Achievement
Selection of Artifacts	All artifacts and work samples are clearly and directly related to the purpose and guidelines of the portfolio and are from a wide range of areas.	Most artifacts and work samples are related to the purpose and guidelines of the portfolio and are from a variety of areas.	Few artifacts and work samples are related to the purpose and/or guidelines of the portfolio and not from a variety of areas.	Most artifacts and work samples are unrelated to the purpose and guidelines of the portfolio and/or are from a limited number of areas.
Quality of Artifacts	The selections are impeccable and show extreme care and thoughtfulness in craftsmanship.	The selections are neat and craftsmanship is good.	The selections are somewhat messy and craftsmanship detracts somewhat from overall presentation.	The selections are messy and craftsmanship detracts from overall presentation.

Criteria	Exemplary Achievement	Proficient Achievement	Developing Achievement	Emerging Achievement
Organization and Technical Control	The artifacts are well organized. There are few or no errors with the conventions.	The artifacts are organized. There are a few errors with the conventions.	The artifacts are not always well-organized. There are a number of errors with the conventions.	The artifacts are disorganized. There are many errors with the conventions.
Reflections	All reflections clearly describe why artifacts in the portfolio demonstrate achievement, growth, and the complexity of the content.	Most of the reflections describe why artifacts in the portfolio demonstrate achievement, growth, and an understanding of the content.	A few reflections describe why artifacts in the portfolio demonstrate achievement, growth, and some understanding of the content.	Reflections are missing, and those that are there do not describe why artifacts in the portfolio demonstrate achievement, growth, and little or no understanding of the content.

Report Cards and Transcripts

As discussed in Chapter 3, there is a myopic focus on grades in today's schools. Many administrators, teachers, students, and families have lost sight of the importance of the mission-based outcomes. By the time students reach middle elementary, they have already figured out the game of grades. When students reach high school, grades become the ticket into colleges and universities, and the pressure students feel is considerable. The college and university admission process has made the student's grade point average (GPA) out to be a primary factor for enrollment decisions. This system has resulted in students being more interested in gaining points in class for a grade than in what is being learned or their self-development.

For teachers who have adopted the Understanding by Design framework and have developed rich performance tasks focused on understanding and/or transfer, it is challenging to shift student mindsets and to generate meaningful grades. Some parents and students who have only experienced the traditional model do not understand that there are other possibilities for schools to design instruction and report on student progress.

A growing group of educators and parents is beginning to question the traditional grading system, which usually ends up with teachers giving students an A, B, C, D, or F at the end of each marking period. Recently, the Association for Supervision and Curriculum Development (ASCD) has given considerable visibility to this topic in both their professional journal, *Educational Leadership*, and through publication of numerous books on changing grading practices.

Tony Wagner and Ted Dintersmith's book *Most Likely to Succeed: Preparing Our Kids for the Innovation Era* spends a considerable amount of time focusing on this issue and how counterproductive the traditional grading system is, as well as how the college and university system perpetrates this system. Also, a group of approximately one hundred high schools, the Mastery Transcript Consortium, is developing an alternative transcript that reflects the unique skills, strengths, and interests of each learner.[5]

From a Christian school perspective, students often are given mixed messages about what is important. If spiritual growth and development is a Christian school's primary purpose, then should not the student reporting system give students feedback about this all-important area? One look at most Christian school K–8 report cards and high school transcripts yields little useful information about a student's spiritual development. The Bible grade is usually little more than a reflection of basic knowledge about the Scriptures, rather than a picture of a student's understanding of complex biblical issues or a student's relationship with Christ and the people around them.

Once a Christian school adopts the UbD framework and begins to see improved student engagement and shifts in focus to mission-related outcomes, the student reporting system invariably surfaces as one of the school's practices that is not well-aligned. Since the current traditional grading practices are considered sacred by many educators, parents, and students, the school's leadership may need to move slowly on this issue.

Rather than tackling only the grading practices issue, it would be wise to look at the whole student reporting system (parent notification channels, homework, progress reports, report cards, conferences, transcripts). Devising a student reporting system that includes information about student progress and growth on the school's priority mission-related outcomes

---

5. https://mastery.org/

should be considered in each area. Homework, report cards, and transcripts are the most challenging aspects, and making changes in these practices is more complicated when going from elementary to middle school and then to high school.[6]

It is critical to involve the full staff in researching and grappling with possible changes to a school's reporting system, to make changes in stages, and to carefully keep parents and students informed about the reasons for your changes. There is no one solution to making changes to a student reporting system. Because every Christian school is unique with its own mission, having staff at each school adopt their own changes is the best approach.

Personnel Practices

Personnel practices include hiring, appraisal, and development of staff. The school's leadership is responsible for hiring personnel and providing training, supervision, and evaluation of staff. In a school that is thinking systemically, hiring staff who support the school's mission is another important obligation.

If the school is mission-driven and has a clear agreement on what quality teaching and learning look like, selecting administrative and teaching staff can be done more intentionally. Clarifying job expectations through job descriptions allows the interview process to focus on the school's mission-based outcomes. Each potential new hire should be given the school mission, graduate outcomes, learning principles, and job descriptions as part of the hiring process. Often in Christian schools, the number of available candidates is limited. So, advertising each position with clear expectations helps in two ways:

- potential candidates who are interested in an instructional program with a strong Christian mission-based focus are likely to apply, and

---

6. There are many articles and books on homework and grading practices. On a national level, Cathy Vatterott, a professor of education at the University of Missouri–St. Louis and a former middle school teacher and principal, has authored four books including *Rethinking Homework: Best Practices That Support Diverse Needs* (ASCD, 2019) and *Rethinking Grading: Meaningful Assessment for Standards Based Learning* (ASCD, 2015). Dr. Thomas Guskey, a senior research scholar in the College of Education and Human Development at the University of Louisville and professor emeritus in the College of Education at the University of Kentucky, has authored/edited twenty-five award-winning books and more than 250 book chapters, articles, and professional papers on educational measurement, evaluation, assessment, grading, and professional learning.

- it gives God a chance to steer the right staff to the school because of the clearly laid out expectations.

Job descriptions can be revised so that they reveal expectations of teaching:

- Create units of instruction using the Understanding by Design framework including teaching for understanding and transfer along with traditional knowledge and skills.

- Assess student performance using a range of assessment practices including performance tasks.

- Professional growth is the expected norm at the school along with collaboration.

Also, the questions used in the interview process should be probing with regards to the candidate's knowledge about current brain research and best practices about teaching and learning. (e.g., What have you been reading professionally over the last few years, and how has it impacted your teaching? What are the key learning principles that guide your belief about quality instruction? Do you understand that high-quality instruction is half the battle when it comes to classroom management? What do you know about differentiation, and what practices have you used in the classroom? What are your beliefs about each student being uniquely made by God, and how does that impact how you approach students?)

The interview process may not result in finding a person who fits all the school's expectations, but at least the person who is hired will know what the expectations are and will later be more likely to rethink and broaden their own instructional practices.

The second area of personnel practices is providing training, supervision, and evaluation of staff. The induction program for all new staff needs to be more than just touring the facility, meeting key staff, being given their textbooks, told where to eat lunch, and make copies. If staff are expected to use UbD framework, then training them is essential along with providing teachers with individuals who can mentor them. The observation process of administrators or teachers should include giving feedback on how they are supporting the school's mission-driven outcomes. Evaluations should have a results-based system section that addresses each individual's ability to meet expectations of a school that requires high-quality instruction and ongoing professional growth.

The last arena of the personnel responsibilities is to provide professional development that addresses current research and best practices. If there are multiple campuses in a Christian school, professional development may need to be tailored for each staff. Every campus has its own culture and readiness level, and a one-size-fits-all approach is often ineffective.

When all three of these areas are working in concert to support a Christian school's mission, the right people join the team, and the school is more effective in achieving its purposes.

Policies and Practices

In addition to the student reporting system, other school practices surface that need to be looked at. School master calendars, school daily schedules, and master schedules can be topics that staff often begin to consider.

How should the master calendar be laid out, if the goal is to have sufficient time for professional growth activities to occur effectively and still meet the state requirements? Do they need full-day and/or half-day release time? How about early-release or late-start options? Could some staff development occur prior to school opening, at the end of the school year, or during existing staff meeting time?

Do the school's beginning and end dates really support achieving the school's mission? Are breaks and vacations and other activities (e.g., conferences, testing, assemblies, field trips) arranged to best support student learning? Are quarters or trimesters best for the school?

Do the daily schedules or the master schedule best support the school's mission-related outcomes? Where are electives placed in the schedule? Do students have breaks for brain rest each day? Is it possible to build a master schedule so specific teachers can regularly collaborate? Do students face too many responsibilities at once several times each year and too few at other times? Should they have seven periods every day, a block schedule, or a modified block schedule?

Do the school's food options support good nutrition? Is there sufficient physical activity planned for all students? Are the school's start and ending times appropriate for the various age groups?

These and other questions invariably arise when a school begins to review current research and best practices. Just as with the student reporting system, it is best to move slowly, research thoroughly, and keep all parties informed as changes are made.

Governance

Governance of Christian schools comes in all kinds of flavors. Most Christian schools have either a governing board that is umbrellaed under a supporting church or an independent school board. The dynamics between the school board and the school's leadership vary greatly.

Trying to balance responsibilities in a Christian school is key to its efficient functioning and being able to establish a culture of school improvement and professional growth.

A good book that outlines an ideal model for schools is Simon Jeynes's *A Call to Authentic Christian School Trusteeship.* He suggests that the board, administration, and faculty and staff should function as partners. The board's primary responsibilities are in strategic planning, financial management, and hiring and supervision of the head of the school. The school's administration is responsible for implementing the mission and vision and orchestrating strategies for achieving the mission. The faculty and staff are responsible for implementation of the school's strategic plan and instruction.

All three of these partners have a part in any Christian school's direction and implementation of new policies or practices. It is important for each either to be informed or to participate in the process of improving the school's instructional program. The head of the school should work with the board on a strategic plan that includes improvement of the instructional program and should regularly give the board updates on progress. The administration should work closely with the teachers and staff as the plan unfolds. Establishing a teacher leader group can be useful in wrestling with complex changes, as it is an excellent forum for professional discussions and distributing responsibilities.

A change process is complex, takes time, and may not unfold according to plan. Invariably, adjustments will need to be made along the way. Having to make modifications does not reflect weak leadership or poor planning, but rather wise leadership. When dealing with this number of people and a school's existing culture, it is not really possible to foresee what will go smoothly and what will need amendment.

Following is an example of a multiyear plan for Christian school improvement.

Schooling by Design: Multiyear Planning Proposal for Three Rivers Christian School

For the past few years, Three Rivers Christian School has been in the process of changing our paradigm for how "Christian Education" should look. The board, administrative team, staff, and stakeholders have all been involved in a process of reevaluating all areas of the school and trying to determine what's most effective in achieving the school's mission. Instead of carrying on the traditional model (which we've sometimes referred to as "public school with a Christian twist"), we've been researching and seeking alternatives based on proven effectiveness.

The Schooling by Design framework has provided, along with the accompanying Understanding by Design training, a systematic direction for our school to define who we are and improve the outcomes of our efforts. In a continuation of that process, we've created the following future plan for further implementation of improvements.

2018–19 School Year Goals	Who	When
Develop Educational Goals/Portrait of a Graduate	Staff/Admin Team	*Completed*—Fall 2018
Implement training for revision of classroom/curriculum methodology (UbD/Project-Based Learning, or PBL)	Staff/Admin Team	Ongoing— 2018–19
Further develop integration and availability of technology in classrooms/staff training • Attend ISTE conference • Digital media class supplies • Chromebooks for elementary • iPad cart • Trial of Promethean panel • Addition of LEGO robotics opportunity	All	*Completed*—2018–19 via funding from local foundation and Weyerhaeuser Foundation
Select new assessment tool (MAP)	Testing Committee	*Completed*—Fall 2018
Develop Principles of Learning	Staff/Admin Team	*Completed*—Winter 2018
Increase assistance for learning-differenced students through development of NILD training and Educational Coaching program	Educational Coach	*Completed*— Fall 2018
Visit other schools in an effort to evaluate different transcript/grading options	Admin Team	Ongoing—Winter 2018/ Spring 2019
Establish resource for additional Bible class training tools/enrichment for teacher access	Admin Team	*Completed*—Winter 2019
Develop new curriculum replacement schedule	Admin Team/Curriculum Leadership Group (CLG)	*Completed*—Winter 2019

2019–20 School Year Goals	Who	When
Develop Curriculum Leadership Group (CLG) • Oversee revision of curriculum maps • Implement curriculum replacement schedule • Continued training to become on-campus "resources" for UbD planning • Align priorities with results from MAP assessments • Implementation of unit Peer Review times • Review of UbD units with principals • Discussion and development of guidelines for homework • Develop Rubrics, Anchors, Exemplars • Determination of standards/proficiencies used for alignment	Admin Team/CLG	Beginning Spring 2018
Develop UbD training for new staff—August	Admin Team/CLG	Spring/Summer 2019
Continue development of UbD units	Admin Team/CLG	2019–20
Complete staff reading on homework philosophy. Begin discussion and evaluation of current homework practices. CLG to draft homework philosophy document based on those discussions.	Admin Team/ CLG Dr. Jan Rauth, Consultant	Summer/Fall 2019
Cornerstone assessment development: Each teacher to establish three rich performance tasks in their class	Staff/Admin Team/ CLG	Beginning Fall 2019
Discussion and evaluation of current conference methods with entire staff. CLG to create a philosophy of student conferences with this information.	Staff/Admin Team/ Curriculum Leadership Group	Beginning Fall 2019

2019–20 School Year Goals	Who	When
Continue development of STEAM-based Agriculture program, and consider schoolwide performance tasks	CLG—Ag Instructor	Beginning Fall 2019
Add next level of LEGO Robotics program	Volunteers Jeanne Nortness/Brice Richards	Fall 2019
Further develop Educational Coaching program with additional training/access to Woodcock Johnson testing and next level of NILD certification	Educational Coach	Summer 2019
Update reporting on assessment to board/stakeholders	Admin Team	Fall 2019
Further develop integration and avail- ability of technology in classrooms/staff training • Supplies for music program • Digital media class supplies • Increased use of Promethean tool in specific classrooms	Staff/Admin Team	Fall 2019
Staff to focus on attributes for portfolio collection. CLG to define portfolio guidelines and train students and staff. Staff to receive training on grading systems. CLG to research and select standards for alignment.	Staff/Admin Team	Winter/Spring 2019
Further develop alumni connection program	Director of Advancement	2019
Begin redesign of teacher evaluation with compensation connected to evalua- tion results	Staff/Admin Team	Winter/Spring 2020

2020–21 School Year Goals	Who	When
Continue work of Curriculum Leadership Group • Oversee completion of curriculum maps—put together accreditation resources • Implement curriculum replacement schedule • Continued training to become on-campus "resources" for UbD planning • Align priorities with results from MAP assessments • Implementation of Unit Peer Review times • Review of UbD units with principals • Continue to collect and develop Rubrics, Anchors, Exemplars	Admin Team/CLG	2020–21
Evaluate and design transition of elementary technology lab to technology "Maker Space"	Staff/Admin Team	Summer 2020
Students and staff trained on portfolio process. Portfolio evidence collection begins.	Staff/Admin Team/ CLG	Summer 2020
Develop Accreditation Leadership Team and begin self-study	Admin Team	Fall 2020
Students and staff trained on portfolio process. Portfolio evidence collection begins.	TRCS Staff/Admin Team	Winter/Spring 2019
Continue development of UbD units	Admin Team/CLG	2020–21
Cornerstone Assessments: CLG group to help establish and evaluate which performance tasks will become cornerstone assessments. Trial-specific assessments.	CLG	Fall 2020

2020–21 School Year Goals	Who	When
Adoption of new student conference model. Evaluation of models.	Staff/CLG	November 2020
Full adoption of homework philosophy in classes	Staff	2020
Update reporting on assessment to board/stakeholders	Admin Team	Fall 2020
Implement redesign of teacher evaluation	Staff/Admin Team	Spring 2021

2021–22 School Year Goals	Who	When
Accreditation Visit	Staff/Admin Team	Fall 2021
Continue work of Curriculum Leadership Group • Oversee completion of curriculum maps—put together accreditation resources • Implement curriculum replacement schedule • Continued training to become on-campus "resources" for UbD planning • Align priorities with results from MAP assessments • Implementation of Unit Peer Review times • Review of UbD units with principals • Continue to collect and develop Rubrics, Anchors, Exemplars	Admin Team/CLG	2021–22
Update reporting on assessment to board/stakeholders	Admin Team	Fall 2021

2021–22 School Year Goals	Who	When
Continue development of UbD units	Admin Team/CLG	2021–22
Cornerstone Assessments: Implementation of further cornerstone assessments in K–12 program.	Staff	Fall 2021

Resources

Maximizing resources is generally one thing that Christian schools do amazingly well. Christian schools do more with less than most other schools—private, charter, or traditional public. Not everything implemented in a strategic plan will require additional resources, but some aspects will. There are times when the Lord provides benefactors for special projects. But over the long haul, in order to sustain a mission-focused culture of professional growth, it will need to be planned for within the annual budget.

Over a multiyear plan, the resource needs will shift. During the early days, staff development will be a focus, and funds may be needed for staff development materials, consultant costs, conferences, school visits, and/or teacher stipends. Further into the process, instructional materials will likely need to be added and/or technology purchased for staff and/or students.

Changes in the teacher induction program, mentor teachers, or teacher leaders may need to be considered. Also, it usually requires a computer programmer to make changes in student report cards.

These and numerous other areas may need resources to effectively conduct changes in an instructional program that focuses on the school's mission.

Key Chapter Takeaways

✓ Systemic thinking is paramount when trying to make significant change to any organization.

✓ Wiggins and McTighe have outlined six areas for systemic thinking for schools: mission and philosophy; learning principles; curriculum and assessment systems; instructional programs and practices; personnel:

hiring, appraisal, and development; and policies, structures, governance, and resources.

✓ Mission and vision along with learning principles are the foundation for the other components of a school's organization.

✓ The likelihood of achieving the mission-related results increases greatly when all six components work in concert.

✓ Change is hard for any organization.

✓ Working a strategic plan by involving key stakeholders in the process, giving time to work through changes, and being willing to adjust along the way increases the chances of students achieving the school's mission.

Concluding Thoughts

In the end, there is no silver bullet when it comes to school improvement. It is helpful to be able to hire a consultant, attend conferences, select and purchase instructional materials, hire quality staff (administrator or teacher), and secure grant funds; however, in reality it is the orchestration of all the major components of a school in concert with the school's mission that results in achieving a school's purposes. Put this together with a staff who looks to the Lord for guidance and prayerfully approaches the change process, and the likelihood of improving the school's instructional program increases dramatically.

> If you always do what you've always done, you'll always get what you've always got.
>
> —HENRY FORD

> God doesn't call the qualified. He qualifies the called.
>
> —MARK BATTERSON

Educator Interview

Q: As a Christian school superintendent, you have
the important responsi-
bility of setting direction
and goals. What has been
your greatest challenge
at your school over the
last few years as you have
made significant changes?

Superintendent

ERIN HART

Bio

ACSI Accreditation Commission
Board Member—Washington
  Federation of Independent
  Schools
Christian School
  Superintendent—6 years

A: The biggest challenge to the
direction we've been mov-
ing is probably communi-
cation. Change absolutely
requires good communica-
tion. Each time we achieve
a goal or revise our direction, we have to make sure

BA, Writing and Communications,
  Evergreen State College
MA, Educational Leadership,
  Concordia University

and bring everyone along with us—staff, students, parents, volunteers.
In any organization, you can always improve and you realize quickly
that you'll never *arrive*. We've learned that the idea of "growth mindset"
is not just for our students, but it applies to our leadership and our organization. To remove ourselves from the industrial model of education is
a real brain-bender for many of our stakeholders.

Managing the message of these changes and making sure that
staff is also able to do so is incredibly important. It's difficult to feel
like you're repeating yourself constantly, but I'm learning that leadership is all about keeping a focus on what your organization wants to
become. Tell everybody about the changes you're making, and when
you're done, find an opportunity to tell them again.

Q: **What impact have brain-based research and best practices had on
your thinking about what a quality education looks like in this
twenty-first century?**

A: It's been an affirmation of many of our moves away from the industrial model of education. From how the classroom is set up to a better understanding of how the brain processes and stores information, this learning has helped reinforce new practices that are sometimes questioned by parents. Most parents believe that the mode of learning ("sit and get") that they grew up with is what they should expect for their children. When the student is moving beyond tests that ask them to "memorize the boldface words," and instead is given performance tasks that require critical thinking, we're able to explain to parents why one is providing more effective and lasting learning than the other. Every area of the classroom can be impacted by brain research: from classroom management to grading practices.

Q: Making systemic change in a school requires thoughtful planning and patience. What has helped you develop a realistic strategic plan that is mission-focused?

A: Designing with the end in mind is applicable in all areas of the school—not just in lesson design. We often thought of our mission and vision in strategic planning, but not with the same level of intentionality that we do now. Going through the practice that helped us break down our educational goals, especially in light of our core values, has given us a lens through which to view every program and practice. In board-level discussions, it gives us a framework to reign in the disparate ideas that may come during the planning process. There may be many good ideas out there—but they may not fit our mission and goals.

Recently our leadership team designed a performance task for our teaching staff. We had them evaluate every program and practice of the school as though they were "storefronts" that they would then have to "sell" to parents. The evaluation tools were our mission, vision, and educational goals. They then had to communicate why they would keep (or jettison) the program. This task developed an ability in our staff to articulate the meaning and value of the work we're doing. Along the way, we've learned that applying backward design isn't just for unit planning, but it's for envisioning the entire work of the school.

Q: How have you kept your school board informed and engaged in the change process at your school?

A: When we initially decided to adopt UbD, the board received some training on the basic concepts and learned some of the common language. They currently receive a monthly report on the progress of our SbD planning, and it's a facet of our overall plan for continuous school improvement. The shift to UbD has also provided us with more meaningful data, both qualitative and quantitative, about student academic progress to share with our board.

Q: **How has your staff reacted to the many changes that have been instituted?**

A: Educators in the past few decades have become skeptics, thanks to the continual merry-go-round of new theories and practices. Our staff was no different in the beginning—but once they realized that UbD wasn't forcing them to use an exact recipe or just adding another tool to their toolbox but instead giving them a framework in which their own creativity and skills could flourish, they started to get excited.

   The hardest part is changing mindsets. This isn't "one more thing to do," but instead helps weed out what's ineffective and helps develop what proves to be lasting, meaningful learning. Being a little scared at the beginning is a rational reaction, but as we've learned from neurologists, the brain works best with a certain amount of stress applied in a meaningful way. That's the same for teachers as for students! It's forced us to work a little harder, but the outcome is so valuable!

Q: **What do you see as needed changes in Christian schools' instructional programs for them to be the most impactful for God's kingdom?**

A: I believe that by virtue of referencing Christ in our name, we should be striving daily to be better than the pattern set by the world. So often, Christian schools have become "public school with a Christian twist." We are replicating the model that trained us instead of using our God-given reason to develop a model of education that is Christ-centered and student-serving. If we deeply consider our individual missions, it doesn't take long to see that much of what we try to accomplish during the school year isn't serving that mission, but instead is checking the boxes of what the world expects for our children. We can't compete with the public schools and their economies of scale, but we can be highly relational in a world that is starved for true connection, and we can offer unique programs that are suited to our individual communities and mission statements. We need to focus on our differentiators to prove our value in the twenty-first century.

Q: **What advice would you give to other Christian school administrators who desire to make significant changes in their Christian school's instructional program?**

A: Be relentless in pursuit of those improvements. So often we tell ourselves that we're stuck because we don't have the money that we believe improvement requires—but I think the adage that "provision follows vision" is true. So many improvements simply require organization, deep thinking, and will—and often those changes attract the attention of people who want to invest in your mission. Investing in your mission is a big difference from what many Christian schools seek in their donors—often a "bridge the gap" mentality of filling a bottomless void.

I also believe in that other adage: "Leaders are readers." There are many great thinkers out there who are writing about futuristic education, brain-based learning, and creative teaching. Many of them are founded in biblical truth, even if they didn't intend it! As Dr. Alan Pue said, "If you want your school to get better, you've got to get better first." I believe that begins with a desire to learn from those who are already doing it well or wrestling creatively with the problems in education.

7

To Change or Not to Change, That Is the Question

Now may our Lord Jesus Christ himself and God our Father,
who loved us and by grace gave us eternal comfort and good hope,
encourage your hearts and strengthen you in
every good thing you do or say.

—2 THESSALONIANS 2:16–17 (NLT)

THE INTENT OF THIS book is to stimulate thinking, conversation, and action of Christian school leaders in how to improve the quality of their schools by being more mission-aligned. Hopefully, the ideas presented here have sparked Christian school leaders' interest to dig deeper into considering changes necessary in today's Christian schools. In this era where education has become as much a political football as an educational endeavor and the world is experiencing rapid change, interest in Christian schools has waned. Christian school leaders have the responsibility of not just maintaining a school, but also of grappling with how to make changes to their schools that will better achieve their mission.

This will require committed Christian school leaders—board members, administrators, and teacher leaders—who understand what God has allowed neuroscience and cognitive psychologists to learn about how the brain learns best and who are willing to work toward making the necessary changes to their instructional program. The research about the brain will never fully unravel all the mysteries that only God knows but will likely continue to reveal information about how the brain works that will aid educators. What has already been learned certainly puts educators on notice that the traditional model of stand-and-deliver instruction will yield less than optimal results.

Even more importantly, David I. Smith postulates in his book *On Christian Teaching: Practicing Faith in the Classroom* that an educator's faith can have impact on their pedagogical practices. He believes faith should shape pedagogy and that more dialogue needs to occur about the relationship between faith and pedagogy. He notes that while there is no single prescriptive model for teaching in Christian schools, how we use space and time, along with the strategies we choose, do impact student learning.

Taking a long-term and systemic approach to making changes will be necessary. There is no simple quick fix to this kind of school improvement. Training staff on the current research and best practices and giving staff time to grow professionally, to implement changes, and to reflectively review their progress is essential. This kind of shift to implement research-informed practices is difficult and iterative, but it is achievable.

Each period of history has its own unique challenges. Regardless of the time period, Christian education should not lose sight of its primary mission of developing spiritually grounded young men and women for the furtherance of God's kingdom.

There are many resources available today for educational leaders to guide the change process. It is my hope that you are encouraged and willing to let God lead you into this endeavor.

This is why we labor and strive, because we have put our hope
in the living God, who is the Savior of all people,
and especially of those who believe.

—1 TIMOTHY 4:10 (NIV)

Postface

Purpose in Life: Investing the treasure of time into that which will
bring the most lasting results.

WHAT MOTIVATED ME TO write this book? First and foremost, I believe
God was prompting me to do so. I have had a blessed educational career,
beginning in 1970. I have served in the majority of roles that exist within
education today: teacher, department chair, assistant principal, principal,
assessment director, assistant superintendent, chair of accreditation teams,
adjunct professor, and educational consultant and coach. When it came
time for me to retire from my last public school position, I decided that I
wanted to give back to Christian education, as I learned a lot about godly
leadership during my first principalship, which was in a Christian high
school. Christ has been the center of most of my adult life, and I do not
really believe that drinking a cup of coffee each morning and reading the
newspaper is what He has called me to do in the latter part of life.

My experience with Understanding by Design began nearly twenty
years ago. I have experienced the power of Grant Wiggins and Jay McTighe's
thoughtful ideas. Over this time, I personally have seen the positive impact
on student learning through individual teachers; on elementary, middle,
and high schools; and on whole school districts. The positive impact has
occurred in traditional public schools, charter schools, and Christian
schools. Also, I am sure if you had the privilege of sitting down with Jay
McTighe, his stories would dwarf my experience.

Therefore, I set aside my public-school consulting work, and after a
brief rest, the Lord found me a Christian school that was in need. A number

of years and several Christian schools later, I came to a point where I saw a broader need within Christian education.

My hope is that this book will stimulate Christian school leaders and teachers to consider the Understanding by Design framework and Schooling by Design principles. The ideas are rooted in what current brain research is telling us about quality teaching and learning. From a Christian perspective, they transcend many of the humanistic-based ideas that exist with the public sector. They provide Christian schools with a road map, set of principles, and common language that can support Christian schools in making the necessary changes to better meet their mission and maximize their impact for God.

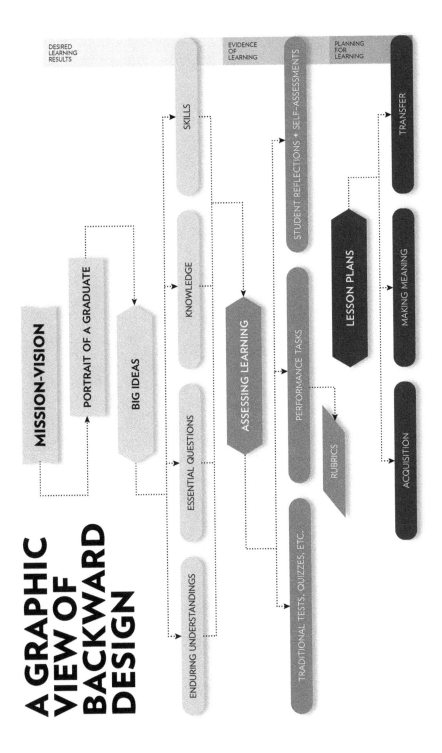

A GRAPHIC
VIEW OF
BACKWARD
DESIGN

MISSION-VISION

PORTRAIT OF A GRADUATE

BIG IDEAS

DESIRED
LEARNING
RESULTS

SKILLS

KNOWLEDGE

ESSENTIAL QUESTIONS

ENDURING UNDERSTANDINGS

EVIDENCE
OF
LEARNING

ASSESSING LEARNING

STUDENT REFLECTIONS + SELF-ASSESSMENTS

PERFORMANCE TASKS

RUBRICS

TRADITIONAL TESTS, QUIZZES, ETC.

PLANNING
FOR
LEARNING

LESSON PLANS

TRANSFER

MAKING MEANING

ACQUISITION

157

Appendix

A Head of School Story

IF YOU'RE CONNECTED TO a Christian school, see if this sounds familiar:

Our school had been around for decades, following a long-ago written mission statement that nobody really knew. We were all about loving God and loving children, and our reputation was not centered on academic excellence, but centered on being a place that felt like "family." A well-intentioned, hard-working group, our staff came from a variety of skill sets and backgrounds but were generally certified or retired teachers who could afford to work for a smaller salary. In the absence of a unifying directive other than our statement of faith, each classroom was a unique reflection of the teacher. Students were learning, but staff was consistently frustrated with being unsure of what was happening in other grade levels and if they were teaching or reteaching the same things. Everyone was wearing a ton of hats. Worry about the budget was pervasive as was the desire to sacrifice salaries and supplies to keep tuition low. Professional development time was generally just for breathing room. The strategic plan was a dusty document on a shelf, full of items that would only be accomplished if somebody who loved the school won the lottery. Each year, we were just grateful to fundraise the shortfall in the budget so we could start all over again. We sent off groups of graduates with hearts for Jesus, but in anonymous alumni interviews, they described memories of a scattershot educational experience, some expressing a remembrance of entire seasons where they memorized a lot but "learned little."

Appendix

If you are part of a Christian school, at least some of what I described above is familiar to you. And if any of it is familiar, you should be as scared as we were. Over a thousand private Christian schools in the United States have closed in the past ten years.

Five years ago, I transitioned from development director of Three Rivers Christian School to the head of school position. In retrospect, I've often wondered if the board just felt like things couldn't get much worse, so they handed a seven-page job description and a school with a six-digit accounts receivable number to the person who had been marginally successful in plugging the fundraising gap for the prior few years. I had a disparate background in marketing, education, culinary arts, and architecture: the one trait I could clearly demonstrate was a capacity to learn. The K–12 principal and I were tasked with plugging the holes in the school's proverbial boat and seeing if we could make her seaworthy once again.

I read Collins, Sinek, and Lencioni. I interviewed all the staff members, and the principal and I made ourselves a promise: Anyone who didn't demonstrate in the interview a passion for serving children *and* a desire to find a better way to do so needed to find a new job. We hired a new business manager—a person who had the grit and passion to grind out the hard changes and help us become auditable. We had amazing donors who came forward to fund specific projects. We plugged holes, cut costs, repaired aging buildings, raised salaries for existing staff, and hired new staff too. We sought out training wherever we could find it, investigating project-based learning and attempting to excite teachers about different ways of assessing and motivating students to learn. We pursued the smart veterans of the Christian schooling movement and tried to iron out our "why," revisiting our mission and vision. We threw out the old strategic plans and built improvement plans with one-year goals and were encouraged when we were able to check the items off the list. We worked like it depended on us and prayed like it depended on God—and then we prayed some more.

Yet we *still* felt like we weren't sure how we were proving our value to parents. I'd joked (only in part) for years that Christian schools were in danger of becoming "Pharisee factories," producing book smart rule followers who lack heart and compassion. As area public schools raced to introduce more programs and technology, we worried that in trying to match them, we were only becoming "public schools with a Christian twist."

We kept wondering, as a Christian school, how do we move beyond platitudes to intentionally and strategically building up the lives of our students? How do we make our mission statement into reality?

Simon Jeynes, one of my favorite thinkers in Christian education, once said at a conference I attended, "Show me your budget and your schedule, and I'll tell you your mission—and it's probably not the one you're advertising in your mission statement." It was convicting, irritating, and undeniably true.

One afternoon, God's grace came in the form of a phone call. Years ago (in my development director role), I had applied for a grant from a private foundation. At the time, we didn't receive the grant—in fact, I didn't blame them for not awarding it to us. Our financials showed us bleeding money, and we had limited quantitative data to show their board what good was coming from our school. However, we had kept the foundation on our e-mail newsletter list, and they had been watching us as we made improvements and tried to push forward.

"We've been watching you report on the changes at your school, and we're really encouraged by your efforts," said the member of the foundation. "Are there any projects we can help you with?"

I can tell you in complete honesty: This was probably the closest I've ever come to fainting. I babbled a bit about needing a new transport van, or maybe some help with scholarships—but the foundation member said they'd read something interesting in our newsletter about how we were trying to move away from "stand and deliver" styles of teaching to a more project-based, student-centered perspective. This foundation had a connection with a veteran educator and consultant who they thought would be a good fit for our school.

When we first sat down with Steve Butler, he shared with us that he felt many Christian schools were lacking a framework for making the focused changes needed to prepare students for a world that's like nothing that's come before it. In his soft-spoken and methodical way, he talked about everything from the neurological underpinnings of learning to the importance of starting with a valid, well-considered mission statement and designing backwards.

In our previous investigations, we had looked at Understanding by Design (UbD) but dismissed it as too difficult or esoteric. We had spent a day showing our teachers training videos that were later described as "excellent sleep aids." We weren't initially sure that there was any way we could convince our teachers that there was value in jettisoning their regular way of doing things for something different. Steve suggested we read a couple of recommended UbD books and talk further.

A skeptic by nature, I kept a notebook next to me while I read, thinking I'd keep a list of points that I disagreed with or areas in which I found fault. Instead, I found a framework for learning that was beautiful in its simplicity. Here are a few reasons why UbD and the overall framework of Schooling by Design resonated with our school:

- *It's driven by your unique mission.* From the creation of your educational goals to the development of your principles of learning, the variety of responses is infinite and custom to you. It's not a script, but a way of implementing your mission strategically through your educational program.

- *It fosters creativity and helps quantify the qualitative.* We've all had those classroom projects that seem like cornerstones of our program—but on closer inspection, we realize they're probably not teaching our children much. They're produced more by the parents than the students. This process has helped our teachers take those creative projects and redesign them in a way that specifically promotes our mission and goals. Our staff and students are becoming rubric masters and are learning our educational goals by heart.

- *It allows for a broad range of teacher personalities to shine.* Every teacher is different, and seldom does one system of classroom management or teaching style fit all of them. As a framework, I've seen a variety of teacher personalities function in their best light with the help of a unit framework.

- *It's applicable to the entire organization.* We've started to approach every issue in the school from a backwards design mindset. From a leadership position, the framework has helped me keep our goals in mind and work systemically to achieve our mission.

- *It's biblical* (Luke 14:28–33). Why would we not "count the cost" and consider the end result desired when we begin a large-scale effort? Yet so often we don't invest the time in being strategic. We throw everything we've got at a problem, exhausting ourselves in the process. When we invest our resources wisely for a determined goal (Matthew 25:14–30) and take strategic risks based on the promises of God, we allow God to work in our schools.

It's been almost two years of asking ourselves uncomfortable questions. Professional development is no longer "teacher catch-up time," but it has become time to work on new units or practice peer review. There is a new language for academic progress and a common vocabulary for what constitutes success in our mission.

Unlike previous iterations of the campus-wide goals that may have "come down from the mountain with Moses," our teaching staff was part of writing our graduate attributes. After researching the neurological underpinnings of how we learn, the staff wrote our "Principles of Learning," clearly determining what we believe are the most important traits of an effective teacher. Our curriculum maps are moving away from being led by the textbook (or sometimes borrowed by the publisher-written map in the back) to being led by what the student needs to know and the most engaging route to get them there. The textbook has become one more tool in the classroom.

If you visited our campuses, you might see the little differences in the "Discovery" and "Expedition" groups in our chapels. The upper-level students might tell you about their recent travels to Cambodia or Ukraine on "Impact Trips." You might watch the kindergarteners as they investigate why the crows drop walnuts on the pavement, or see the agriculture classes learning about irrigation as they prepare this year's pumpkin crop. You'd see high-school students engaged in performance tasks that were designed without any parent help, as we've become a school that eschews homework (based on the most recent research). All of these little changes are helping our students grow and learn in quantifiably positive ways—and our enrollment is growing as a result, allowing us to expand the reach of our mission to more students. As we approach another accreditation visit in the coming year, we're excited to show the changes on our campuses and to share the shift in engagement. We know who we are and what we want to become, and it's not about a building initiative or a fancy piece of technology. We are driven by the quality of learning and beauty of our educational goals.

We're aware that we may never arrive. We aren't the school we were three years ago, and in three more years we'll look different again. We no longer struggle with a starvation mentality, but we see God's abundance in provision as we're faithful to these improvements. Our emphasis is on the student and their engagement in learning, and we realize that our blessing as a private school is that we are not beholden to any bureaucracy, but we can follow brain-based research and best practices with a biblical mindset. What a gift!

In Christian schools, we know why we need to change: We're trying to educate our children for a world that doesn't exist yet, and we're often replicating a broken industrial model in our schools. It's *how* we change that is often the more difficult question, and one where the framework of UbD has been game-changing for our school.

—Erin Hart

Illustration Credits and Acknowledgments

Cover design by Kat and André Willem Gooren
Cover image by Mark Cruzat
Internal illustrations by André Willem Gooren adapted from ASCD Publications' original designs.

ASCD Publications:

1.	Title:	*Teaching with the Brain in Mind, 2nd Edition*
	Author(s):	Eric Jensen
	Selection:	Guidelines for Direct Instruction of New Content (page 37)
	Credit:	From *Teaching with the Brain in Mind, 2nd Edition,* by Eric Jensen, Alexandria, VA: ASCD. © 2005 by ASCD. Reprinted with permission. All rights reserved.
2.	Title:	*Teaching with the Brain in Mind, 2nd Edition*
	Author(s):	Eric Jensen
	Selection:	Variations of Repetition (page 39)
	Credit:	From *Teaching with the Brain in Mind, 2nd Edition,* by Eric Jensen, Alexandria, VA: ASCD. © 2005 by ASCD. Reprinted with permission. All rights reserved.

Illustration Credits and Acknowledgments

ASCD Publications:

3.	Title:	*Teaching with the Brain in Mind, 2nd Edition*
	Author(s):	Eric Jensen
	Selection:	The Schedule of Complex Learning (page 43)
	Credit:	From *Teaching with the Brain in Mind, 2nd Edition,* by Eric Jensen, Alexandria, VA: ASCD. © 2005 by ASCD. Reprinted with permission. All rights reserved.
4.	Title:	*Upgrade Your Teaching: Understanding by Design Meets Neuroscience*
	Author(s):	Jay McTighe and Judy Willis
	Selection:	Deep Understanding (pages 27–28)
	Credit:	From *Upgrade Your Teaching: Understanding by Design Meets Neuroscience,* by Jay McTighe and Judy Willis, Alexandria, VA: ASCD. © 2019 by ASCD. Reprinted with permission. All rights reserved.
5.	Title:	*Understanding by Design, 2nd Edition*
	Author(s):	Grant Wiggins and Jay McTighe
	Selection:	Curricular Priorities and Assessment Methods (page 170)
	Credit:	From *Understanding by Design, 2nd Edition,* by Jay McTighe and Grant Wiggins, Alexandria, VA: ASCD. © 2005 by ASCD. Reprinted with permission. All rights reserved.
6.	Title:	*Schooling by Design*
	Author(s):	Grant Wiggins and Jay McTighe
	Selection:	Schooling by Design Key Elements (page 6)
	Credit:	From *Schooling by Design,* by Jay McTighe and Grant Wiggins, Alexandria, VA: ASCD. © 2007 by ASCD. Reprinted with permission. All rights reserved.

Illustration Credits and Acknowledgments

ASCD Publications:

7.	Title:	*Integrating Differentiated Instruction and Understanding by Design*
	Author(s):	Carol Ann Tomlinson and Jay McTighe
	Selection:	Applying Differentiation to the UbD° Framework (page 36)
	Credit:	From *Integrating Differentiated Instruction and Understanding by Design*, by Carol Ann Tomlinson and Jay McTighe, Alexandria, VA: ASCD. © 2006 by ASCD. Reprinted with permission. All rights reserved.
8.	Title:	*Understanding by Design Workbook*
	Author(s):	Grant Wiggins and Jay McTighe
	Selection:	UbD: Stages of Backward Design (page 12)
	Credit:	From *Understanding by Design Workbook,* by Jay McTighe and Grant Wiggins, Alexandria, VA: ASCD. © 2004 by ASCD. Reprinted with permission. All rights reserved.

About the Author

STEVEN BUTLER IS MARRIED with four children and five grandchildren. He attended Eastern Michigan University, where he earned a Bachelor of Science in Mathematics and Chemistry, a Master of Arts in Secondary Curriculum, and Educational Specialist in Educational Leadership.

Steven has had a rich set of educational experiences and a long-term commitment to Christ, which have given him a unique perspective of the challenges that Christian schools face today. He has been an educator for over forty-five years, having served as a teacher, elementary and secondary schools principal in both the public and Christian school sectors, assessment director, and assistant superintendent. In addition, he has served on both Christian school and church boards. He has been an adjunct professor, accreditation chair, and educational consultant and is an experienced school-improvement specialist with a demonstrated history of success in assisting schools.

Email: steven.butler-eds@outlook.com
Website: www.stevenbutler-eds.com

Bibliography

Batterson, Mark. *In a Pit with a Lion on a Snowy Day: How to Survive and Thrive When Opportunity Roars.* New York: Multnomah, 2006.

Bodizs, Robert, et al. "Sleep-Dependent Hippocampal Slow Activity Correlates with Waking Memory Performance in Humans." *Neurobiology of Learning and Memory,* 78 (2002) 441–57.

Bradley, Margaret M., and Peter J. Lang. "Measuring Emotion: Behavior, Feeling, and Physiology." In R. D. Lane & L. Nadel (Eds.). *Cognitive Neuroscience of Emotion.* Series in Affective Science, 242–76. Oxford University Press, 2000.

Bransford, John D., et al. *How People Learn: Brain, Mind, Experience, and School,* National Academy of Sciences, 2000.

Brookhart, Susan M. *How to Create and Use Rubrics: For Formative Assessment and Grading.* Alexandria, VA: ASCD, 2013.

Bruner, Jerome. *The Process of Education,* Harvard University Press, 1960.

Cahill, Larry, et al. "Adrenergic activation and memory for emotional events." *Nature* 371 (1994) 702–4.

———. "Enhanced Human Memory Consolidation with Post-Learning Stress: Interaction with the Degree of Arousal at Encoding." *Learning and Memory* 10(4) (2003) 270–74.

Capone, Neal. "K-12 Christian School Sustainability: Leadership Practices." St. John Fisher College Dissertation, 2016.

Clark, Courtney M., and Robert A. Bjork. "When and Why Introducing Difficulties and Errors Can Enhance Instruction." In V. A. Benassi, C. E. Overson, and C. M. Hakala (Eds.), *Applying the Science of Learning in Education: Infusing Psychological Science into the Curriculum,* 2014. 20–30.

Cohen, Gene D. *The Mature Mind: The Positive Power of the Aging Brain.* New York: Basic, 2006.

Cooper, Frank R., et al. *The Biochemical Basis of Neuropharmacology,* 7th edition. New York: Oxford University Press, 1996.

Dement, William C. "Adolescent Sleep." https://web.stanford.edu/~dement/adolescent.html.

Donovan, R. H., and G. M. Andrew. "Plasma B-endorphin Immunoreactivity during Graded Cycle Ergometry." *Medicine and Science in Sport and Exercise* 19(3) (1987) 231.

Druker, Peter F. *Managing the Non-Profit Organization: Practices and Principles.* New York: HarperCollins, 1990.

Bibliography

Fitzpatrick, Joan B. *Why Christian Schools Close: A Model*. Virginia Beach, VA: Regent University, 2002.

Frank, Marcos G., et al. "Sleep Enhances Plasticity in the Developing Visual Cortex." *Neuron* 30(1) (2001) 275–87.

Frost, Gene. "Does Your Christian School Have a Future?" *Christian School Educators* (18)3 (2014–15) 6–8.

————. *Learning from the Best: Growing Greatness that Endures in the Christian School, Volume Two*. Colorado Springs: Purposeful Design, 2015.

Goda, Yukiko, and Graeme Davis. "Mechanisms of Synapse Assembly and Disassembly." *Neuron* 40(2) (2003) 243–64.

Goodrich, Heidi. "Understanding Rubrics." *Educational Leadership* 54(4) (1996–97) 14–17.

Heath, Chip, and Dan Heath. *The Power of Moments*. New York: Simon and Schuster, 2017.

Hunt, Thomas C., and James C. Carper. *The Praeger Handbook of Faith-Based Schools in the United States, K-12, Volume 1*. Praeger, 2012.

Jensen, Eric. *Teaching with the Brain in Mind, 2nd Edition*. Alexandria, VA: ASCD, 2005.

Jeynes, Simon. *A Call to Authentic Christian School Trusteeship*. Xulon, 2017.

Kelso, J. A. Scott. *Dynamic Patterns: The Self-Organization of Brain and Behavior*. Bradford, 1997.

Lankes, Anna Maria D. "Electronic Portfolios: A New Idea in Assessment." *ERIC Digest* (1995) 1–6.

LeDoux, Joseph E. "Emotion, Memory and the Brain." *Scientific American* 270(6) (1994) 50–57.

Lowrie, Row W., Jr. *To Those Who Teach in Christian Schools*. Colorado Springs: Association of Christian Schools International, 1978.

Marzano, Robert J. *What Works in Schools: Translating Research into Action*. Alexandria, VA: ASCD, 2003.

McTighe, Jay, and Harvey F. Silver. *Teaching for Deeper Learning: Tools to Engage Students in Meaning Making*. ASCD, 2020.

McTighe, Jay, and Grant Wiggins. *Essential Questions: Opening Doors to Student Understanding*. Alexandria, VA: ASCD, 2013.

————. *Understanding by Design: Professional Development Workbook*. Alexandria, VA: ASCD, 2004.

McTighe, Jay, and Judy Willis. *Upgrade Your Teaching: Understanding by Design Meets Neuroscience*. Alexandria, VA: ASCD, 2019.

Meece, Judith L., et al. "Predictors of Math Anxiety and its Influence on Young Adolescents' Course Enrollment Intentions and Performance in Mathematics." *Journal of Educational Psychology* 82(1) (1990) 60–70.

Moskovitch, Morris. "Recovered Consciousness: A Hypothesis Concerning Modularity and Episodic Memory." *Journal of Clinical and Experimental Neuropsychology* 17(2) (1995) 276–90.

Nichols, Vance. "Now or Never: The Research Basis for Innovation in Christian Schools." https://cace.org/2018/09/20/now-or-never-the-research-basis-for-innovation-in-christian-schools/.

————. "Schools at Risk: An Analysis of Factors Endangering the Evangelical Christian School Movement in America. PhD Dissertation, University of Southern California, 2016.

Bibliography

Piegneux, Phillipe, et al. "Sleeping Brain, Learning Brain. The Role of Sleep for Memory Systems." *NeuroReport* 12(18) (2001) 111–24.

Prensky, Marc. "Our Brains Extended." Technology-Rich Learning. *Educational Leadership* 70(6) (2013) 22–27.

Ritzema, Rohn. Regional Director's Report. Presentation, Southern California District 4 meeting, California/Hawaii region of the Association of Christian Schools International Temecula, CA: October 2013.

Sanes, Joshua R., and Jeff W. Lichtman. "Induction, Assembly, Maturation, and Maintenance of a Postsynaptic Apparatus." *Nature Reviews Neurology* 2(11) (2001) 791–805.

Schacter, Daniel L. "Priming and Multiple Memory Systems." *Journal of Cognitive Neuroscience* 4(3) (1992) 244–56.

Scherer, Marge. "How and Why Standards Can Improve Student Achievement: A Conversation with Robert J. Marzano." *Educational Leadership* 59(1) (2001) 14–18.

Schroth, Marvin L. "The Effects of Delay of Feedback on a Delayed Concept Formation Transfer Task." *Contemporary Educational Psychology* 17(1) (1992) 78–82.

Schultz, Wolfram, et al. "A Neural Substrate of Prediction and Reward." *Foundations in Social Neuroscience* 275 (2002) 1593–99.

Senge, Peter M. *The Fifth Discipline: The Art and Practice of the Learning Organization.* New York: Doubleday, 2006.

Shimamura, Arthur P. "Relational Binding in Theory and Role of Consolidation of Memory Retrieval." *Neuropsychology* (2002) 61–72.

Smith, David I. *On Christian Teaching: Practicing Faith in the* Classroom. Grand Rapids: Eerdmans, 2018.

Stickgold, Robert, James, et al. "Visual Discrimination Learning Requires Sleep: After Training." *Nature Neuroscience* 3(12) (2000) 1237–38.

Strauch, Barbara. *The Secret Life of the Grown-up Brain: The Surprising Talents of the Middle-Aged Mind.* Viking, 2010.

Swaner, Lynn E., et al. *Mindshift: Catalyzing Change in Christian Education.* Colorado Springs: Association of Christian Schools International, 2019.

Tomlinson, Carol Ann. *How to Differentiate Instruction in Mixed-Ability Classrooms.* Alexandria, VA: ASCD, 2001.

Tomlinson, Carol Ann, and Jay McTighe. *Integrating Differentiated Instruction and Understanding by Design.* Alexandria, VA: ASCD, 2006.

Wagner, Tony, and Ted Dintersmith. *Most Likely to Succeed: Preparing Our Kids for the Innovation Era.* New York: Scribners, 2016.

Whitman, Glenn, and Ian Kelleher. *Neuroteach: Brain Science and the Future of Education.* Lanham, VA: Rowan and Littlefield, 2016.

Willis, Judy. *Brain-Friendly Strategies for the Inclusion Classroom.* Alexandria, VA: ASCD, 2007.

———. *Research-based Strategies to Ignite Student Learning.* Alexandria, VA: ASCD, 2006.

Wiggins, Grant, and Jay McTighe. *Understanding by Design.* Alexandria, VA: ASCD, 1998.

———. *Understanding by Design. 2nd Edition,* Alexandria, VA: ASCD, 2005.

———. *The Understanding by Design Guide to Advanced Concepts in Creating and Reviewing Units.* Alexandria, VA: ASCD, 2012.

———. *The Understanding by Design Guide to Creating High Quality Units.* Alexandria, VA: ASCD, 2011.

Index

Index

Index

Index

Index

Index

Index

CPSIA information can be obtained
at www.ICGtesting.com
Printed in the USA
FSHW022024200321
79600FS

9 781725 28